Anonymous

Roster of Connecticut Volunteers Who Served in the War

Between the United States and Spain

Anonymous

Roster of Connecticut Volunteers Who Served in the War Between the United States and Spain

ISBN/EAN: 9783744687614

Printed in Europe, USA, Canada, Australia, Japan

Cover: Foto ©ninafisch / pixelio.de

More available books at **www.hansebooks.com**

ROSTER

OF

Connecticut Volunteers

WHO

. SERVED IN THE WAR

BETWEEN

The United States and Spain

1898-1899

Published by the Adjutant-General

Hartford Press
THE CASE, LOCKWOOD & BRAINARD COMPANY
1899

MUSTER ROLL

First Regiment Connecticut Volunteer Infantry.

Mustered at Niantic, May 17–18, 1898.

Field and Staff.

Colonel. Charles L. Burdett, ...	Hartford.
Lieutenant-Colonel Andrew G. Hammond, . .	Ft. Leavenworth, Kas.
Major John Hickey, ...	So. Manchester.
Major Edward Schulze, ...	Hartford.
Captain and Adjutant Jonathan M. Wainwright, .	Hartford.
1st Lieutenant and Regimental Quartermaster Arthur H. Bronson, ...	Hartford.
1st Lieutenant and Battalion Adjutant Patrick J. Cosgrove, ...	Hartford.
1st Lieutenant and Battalion Adjutant Frank E. Johnson, ...	Hartford.
Major and Surgeon Thomas F. Rockwell, . .	Rockville.
1st Lieutenant and Assistant Surgeon Richard S. Griswold, ...	Hartford.
1st Lieutenant and Assistant Surgeon John B. McCook,	Hartford.
Chaplain Henry H. Kelsey, ...	Hartford.

Non-Commissioned Staff.

Regimental Sergeant Major Edward E. Moseley, Hartford. Promoted to 1st Lieutenant.

Battalion Sergeant Major John D. Milne, Rockville.

Battalion Sergeant Major Thomas J. Hines, Hartford.

Quartermaster-Sergeant Otto Mantei, Hartford.

Commissary-Sergeant Albert N. Prescott, Hartford. Promoted to 2d Lieutenant.

Hospital Steward Edward C. Noonan, Hartford.

Hospital Steward Lorens J. Madsen, Hartford.

Hospital Steward Wm. B. L. Robertson, Hartford.

Principal Musician John U. B. Thomas.

Chief Musician Thomas J. Kennedy, Gloversville, N. Y.

Principal Musician Charles W. Pierce.

Company A, of Hartford.

Mustered into the U. S. Service, May 17, 1898.

Captain James C. Bailey.

1st Lieutenant Edwin E. Lamb.

2d Lieutenant Charles F. Wolf.

1st Sergeant Frank J. Williams.

Quartermaster-Sergeant George M. Rohrmayer.

Sergeant Joseph R. Neddo.

Sergeant George A. Roemer.

Sergeant Wm. H. Leslie.

Sergeant Charles Olschefskie.

Corporal John G. Libutzke.

Corporal Edward N. Flood.

Corporal Charles S. Riley.

Corporal Eugene J. Sullivan.

Corporal Nick Fredrickson.

Corporal Charles W. Fritzson.

Musician Clinton L. Steele.

Artificer Howard Leslie.
Wagoner Clinton H. Myers.
Musician John W. Lehnemann. (Died of typhoid fever, September 24th.)

Privates.

Blake, Frank
Bennett, Thomas A.
Brant, Fred
Brennan, Wm. J. J.
Bride, Edward, East Hampton.
Bush, Simon J.
Becker, Frederick
Bleasius, Wm. P.
Buell, John A.
Canales, Fred
Campbell, Wm. A.
Cashman, James, Meriden.
Carlson, Otto
Crane, Frank
Claffy, Frank
Coffey, James J.
Daly, John J.
Dolbeare, Wm. B.
Dooley, Timothy
Daniels, Frank D.
D'Arche, Raoul. Promoted to Corporal.
Fargo, Theodore C.
Fuller, Jas. J.
Freund, Simon
Fogg, Wade H.
Gaffey, Wm. F.
Gallivan, Murty J.
Gates, Benjamin
Gropp, Frank
Guckin, Thomas
Green, Samuel W. Promoted to Corporal.
Garland, Frank
Hanson, Harry J.
Harkins, Fred B.
Herter, Louis A.
Heffernan, James
Hindley, George A.
Holt, Rodney A. Discharged August 16, 1898, disability.
Hoban, Edward A.
Holden, John F.
Holmes, Marion S.
Iffland, Alexander
Kalber, Conrad C. Promoted to Corporal.
Kennedy, Patrick D. Promoted to Corporal.
Kilmartin, John. Promoted to Corporal.
Kilmartin, Edward J.
Kostembader, Fred.
Kollenz, Christian
Kenefick, Thomas

Lotze, Frederick
McAdams, Thomas J.
Miller, Richard
Munsell, Wm. F.
Muhleib, Wm. H.
Mullaney, John J.
Mills, Frank
Mitchell, Wm. H.
McQuillen, John J.
O'Brien, Joseph F.
O'Brien, Daniel J.
Parker, Howard
Payne, Herbert R.
Pasco, Arthur J. Transferred to Band.
Palmer, John, Worcester, Mass.
Patton, Benj. S., So. Glastonbury.
Preisner, Arnold, Jr.
Ross, Fred H.
Roulston, Archibald W.
Ryan, James B.
Rivers, Albert
Roehm, Emil W.
Rose, Chas. E.
Roth, Henry
Smith, Edmund S.
Stedman, John E.
Stephan, Maurice
Shapiro, Samuel. Transferred to band.
Steele, Henry W.
Schiessl, Max
Seymour, Edward S. Transferred to band.
Schwerdtfeder, Henry. Transferred to band.
Sullivan, John E.
Tripp, Harold W.
Turner, Wm. A.
Vinton, Wm. O.
Welles, Ralph G.
Westcott, Alexander T. Promoted to Corporal.
Waldo, Leon J.
Wodal, John F.
Young, Wm. H.

Company B, of Hartford.

Mustered into the U. S. Service, May 17, 1898.

Captain John F. Moran.
1st Lieutenant Frank E. Shea.
2d Lieutenant Patrick A. Farrell.
1st Sergeant John J. McMahon.
Quartermaster-Sergeant John F. Dahill.
Sergeant John A. Barlow.
Sergeant George W. Covey.
Sergeant Thomas I. Crilly.
Sergeant Frank H. Lee.
Corporal Thomas F. Gibbons.
Corporal George R. Krull.

Corporal Thomas F. Hogan.
Corporal John T. Blake.
Corporal Edward J. Cosgrove.
Musician Wm. E. Missel.
Musician John Sullivan, Fall River, Mass.
Artificer Wm. A. Doyle.
Wagoner Chas. H. Welton.

Privates.

Aninger, Benj. C.
Abbott, Wm. H., Poquonock.
Bernard, Isadore
Burby, John A.
Burke, Patrick J.
Brust, Frank
Blake, Charles L.
Bogue, Phillip L., New London.
Barrows, Michael
Brooks, William
Brennan, Michael
Belisle, Tancrede
Beaune, Edward P.
Bennett, Lewis J., Poquonock.
Coyle, Frank P.
Collins, Frank W.
Corrigan, John F. Transferred to Hospital Corps, U. S. A.
Clarkin, Peter A.
Cole, Henry J.
Camp, George W.
Cleary, Thomas
Duffy, James A.
Darrow, Nelson E., Guilford. Transferred to band. Enlisted Co. E, 3d C. V. I., January 6, 1899. Transferred to band, 3d C. V. I.
Dougherty, John J.
Devoy, Michael F., Waterbury.
Degnan, James F.
Eagan, John
Finigan, Patrick. Promoted to Corporal.
Ferguson, Owen J.
Fox, Martin J.
Foley, Daniel
Flint, Houston, East Hampton. Transferred to band.
Fox, Oscar, Hazardville.
Frost, Lannie A., Watertown.
Gorman, John J.
Geary, Patrick J.
Gallagher, Patrick
Gasser, Florent, Jr., Torrington.
Hefferman, Charles C.
Henson, Stephen F. Promoted to Corporal.
Hurley, Wm.
Kelly, James
Kershaw, Wm.
Kelley, James J.

Kennedy, James
Kuhn, Albert
Kiely, Abraham
Lewis, George
Little, Harry R.
Lutz, Frank G.
Livingston, Wm. F.
Laughlin, Robert
Lynch, James
Liebert, George S. Promoted to Corporal.
Leonard, Martain C. Deserted.
Maynard, Anson H.
McLaughlin, John J.
McLaughlin, Richard F., Waterbury.
McCarthy, Thomas A.
McAuliffe, James. Promoted to Corporal.
Missel, Jacob J.
Meara, Wm. F.
Murray, Bernard W.
Murray, Luke T.
Murphy, Michael T.
Mooney, Matthew
Murphy, Patrick J.
Malley, Thomas P.
Nolan, Wm. F.
O'Toole, Richard
Payne, Frederick E.
Quirk, Patrick H.
Quinn, Edward W.
Richard, Don C.
Riordon, James I. Promoted to Corporal.
Riedel, Rudolph C.
Riordan, Michael F.
Ryan, Thomas C., Meriden.
Rosheck, Joseph
Scanlan, Thomas J. Promoted to Corporal.
Shannon, Owen
Smith, George H.
Stannard, Clarence H., Guilford. Transferred to band.
Stanley, Joseph T.
Thompson, Walter. Promoted to Corporal.
Williams, Frederick E.
Williams, John H.
Walsh, John J.
Wadsworth, George N.

Company C, of Rockville.

Mustered into the U. S. Service, May 17, 1898.

Captain Martin Laubscher.
1st Lieutenant John Paul Haun.
2d Lieutenant Frederick W. Chapman.
1st Sergeant James H. Barnett.

Quartermaster-Sergeant Francis Murray.

Sergeant Charles B. Milne.
Sergeant Arthur W. Gyngell.
Sergeant James W. Milne. (Died September 26th.)
Sergeant Albert E. Usher.
Corporal William F. Schillinger.
Corporal Webster Kaye.
Corporal William M. Hefferon, Ellington.
Corporal Arthur R. Gerick.
Corporal William J. Breen.
Corporal Albert E. M. Profe.
Musician William J. Finley. Transferred to band.
Musician Walter F. McCray.
Artificer Henry M. Seipt.
Wagoner George B. McClellan, Ellington.

Privates.

Arnold, Sylvester E.
Austin, Ernest E.
Aborn, George N., Ellington,
Anderson, Charles R.
Beaumont, James A.
Brache, Richard
Breen, Frank S.
Broll, Hugo
Brown, Harry J.
Bartlett, Albert C.
Binck, Charles E., New Britain.
Cahoon, Elmer W., North Coventry.
Chadwick, Frank D.
Champion, Richard G.
Charter, Perlin L., Ellington.
Charter, Wilbur F.
Clift, Jesse
Connors, John, 2d
Cullumn, Jewett
Connolly, William J.
Diedering, Philip, Jr.
Donovan, John, Hartford.
Dowd, Frank P., Broadbrook.
Einsiedel, Francis F.
Farrell, James B.
Fitzpatrick, Francis P.
Flynn, Joseph H.
Franz, Herman P.
Flossback, Otto
Fox, David E., Essex.
Gorham, George F.
Gawtrey, John E.
Gross, Felix. (Died September 25th.)
Grumback, Manville
Golden, Thomas F., Hartford.
Haun, John F., Tolland.
Hecker, John J.
Hewett, George A.
Hewett, John A. (Disc. August 11th, disability.

Hopf, Andrew
Jackson, Squire
Jones, James S. Promoted to Corporal.
Jennings, Elijah W., Hartford.
Jepson, John, Hartford.
Lehmann, Robert H., Ellington.
Lowell, Jason D.
Ludwig, Charles F.
Lutton, James H.
Lutz, Joseph H.
Leaney, Martin T., Hartford.
Lyons, William E., Hartford.
Lynch, Thomas P.
Macnamara, Matthew
Mahr, Phillip J.
Matthewson, Ferdinand A.
Meyer, George
Miller, George H.
Moore, Thomas F.
Murphy, John C.
McLagan, Donald K.
Millott, Thomas L.
Manion, Frank L., Hartford.
Murphy, John L., Essex.
Murphy, John W., Hartford.
Murphy, William C., Windsor.
McCullough, Patrick J., Hartford.
Nahigis, Matthew N.
Norton, Francis M.
Newbury, Thomas F.
O'Neil, John J.
Phillips, William
Profe, Frederick J. A. H.
Quinn, James J.
Rau, Robert H.
Raushenback, Charles H., Broadbrook.
Regan, John.
Roche, John J., Hartford.
Scherwitzky, Emil R.
Schmeiske, Carl C.
Schmeiske, Emil W.
Sharp, Ernest A. Transferred to band.
Simms, Isaac
Smith, John H.
Stengel, Frederick W.
Tracy, Henry H., Vernon Center.
Wagner, Herman C.
Wardner, Charles J., Ellington.
Wannenger, Anthony
Willis, Walter J.
Winchell, Howard

Company D, of New Britain.

Mustered into the U. S. Service, May 17, 1898.

Captain Sidney M. Leonard.
1st Lieutenant Louis V. Shutz. Res. ac., to date September 28th.
2d Lieutenant George B. Gifford.

1st Sergeant Eugene F. Barnes.
Quartermaster-Sergeant George W. Barnes.
Sergeant Carl E: Thorngran.
Sergeant James P. Connelly.
Sergeant Walter S. Belden, Plainville. (Died October 28th.)
Sergeant George B. Pickop.
Corporal Frederick G. Beh.
Corporal Harry A. Norton.
Corporal Samuel C. Davis.
Corporal Arthur F. Mitchell.
Corporal Edward J. Sheehy.
Musician John J. Laverty.
Musician William R. Banks, New London.
Artificer Hinman L. Smith, Plainville.
Wagoner Perry Strong.

Privates.

Abrahamson, John W.
Abetz, William
Adolfson, Charles D.
Anderson, Charles F.
Barnes, Wm. H.
Birmingham, Austin A. Promoted to Corporal.
Bloom, Emil G.
Burns, John F. Promoted to Corporal.
Carlson, Victor. Promoted to Corporal.
Cannell, Richard. Promoted to Corporal.
Conlin, Martin E.
Curtis, Edwin S.
Chichester, Burton J.
Canfield, Charles V. J.
Carlson, Jacob
Chapman, Lorenzo B.
Cosgrove, James J.
Coleman, Michael
Cornell, Cornelius H., New London.
Casey, Thomas E., Burnside.
Corbett, Edward J.
Carlson, John E.
Cragan, Charles A., Hartford.
Degnan, Patrick J.
Degnan, Charles
Daly, Michael, Southington.
Devitt, Patrick
Donnellan, Frank P., Buckland. Transferred to Company G June 1, 1898.
Dunbar, Eugene A., Hartford.
Egan, Edward F.
Finochietti, Nicholas
Fritz, George J.
Fritz, Jacob F.
Freese, Ernest W.
Fox, Ernest
Frawley, James
Grady, James J., Hartford.

Graham, John F., Plainville.
Grant, John R., Brockton, Mass.
Hesse, Albert W.
Higgins, Peter J.
Heiderich, Ernest. Deserted.
Hardy, Ernest F., Bristol.
Johnson, Charles G., Plainville.
Johnson, Edward T., Plainville.
Jubb, James
Jones, Charles J.
Kennedy, George P.
Krebser, Frederick, Cambridge, Vt.
Keegan, Allan M. Promoted to Corporal.
Lawton, Albert E.
Larson, Laurin
Lyman, Mortimer. Promoted to Corporal.
McMahon, Peter H.
McMahon, Charles W., Middletown.
McCarthy, John F.
McManus, Thomas A., New London.
May, William
Mulheam, Patrick J., Burnside.
McClellan, William A., East Hartford.
McElrath, James B.
Martin, James F.
McDermott, John
Newton, Ralph J.
O'Connell, John
O'Brien, Simon, South Glastonbury.
O'Brien, William P.
O'Connell, William A., Hartford.
Olson, Albert
O'Conner, Thomas F., Jr.
Potter, Archer I., Plainville.
Parsons, Lester
Palmer. Lewis B.
Post, Samuel
Prentise, George H.
Quinn. John J., Bristol.
Reed, William W. Transferred to band.
Rehm, William F.
Ryan, Thomas J., Berlin.
Russell, Frank E., Plainville.
Spindler, Philip
Schmidt, William J.
Strickland, George N. Promoted to Corporal.
Shea, John J.
Stiles, John F., Meriden.
Staubly, George L., Norwich.
Stanton. Daniel H.
Smith, Fred B.
Shine, Cornelius M.
Urban, Rudolf
Williams, Elmer H.
Wetherill. Joseph A.
Wondruska, Frank. Transferred to band.
Wood, Arthur, Hartford.

8

Company E, of New Britain.

Mustered into the U. S. Service, May 18, 1898.

Captain Abraham L. Hauerwas.
1st Lieutenant George Arthur Hadsell, Plainville.
2d Lieutenant George M. Mycroft.
1st Sergeant John E. Lynch, Meriden.
Quartermaster-Sergeant William W. Bullen, Plainville.
Sergeant Charles A. Anderson.
Sergeant Frederick Gustafson.
Sergeant Louis J. Brague.
Sergeant Burton C. Morey.
Corporal William J. Rice.
Corporal Thomas J. Boyle.
Corporal Ira B. Leonard.
Corporal William T. Young.
Corporal William G. Hall.
Corporal Frank L. Smith.
Artificer George Hoffman.
Wagoner Patrick J. Whalen, Bristol.
Musician Louis A. Kumm. Relieved as musician June 25, 1898.
Musician Axel E. Samuelson.

Privates.

Anderson, Charles
Anderson, Charles A.
Beckett, William H.
Bresnehan, Thomas
Bacon, William, Hartford.
Balf, Edward, Jr., Hartford.
Blakesley, Charles P., Musician.
Brown, George H., Hartford.
Bronkie, Frederick, Manchester.
Callahan, Daniel
Callender, Edward T., Plainville.
Clark, Alpha A.
Cowles, John H., East Hartford.
Coons, Charles, Bristol.
Conner, Norman G., Marshallton, Pa.
Connahan, Daniel J.
Crowe, Luke
Crowe, Luke J.
Carlson, David. (Died October 15th.)
Crowe, Matthew
Casey, Michael J.
Denn, William
Donahue, John J. (Died October 22d.)
Doughty, Alonzo
Duprey, Frank E.
Eades, John A. Promoted to Corporal.
English, Charles R.
Evans, Frederick, Lawrence, Mass.
Fagan, Thomas F.
Fagan, Franklin R. Transferred to Company I.
Finley, George L.

Foley, Thomas
Frechette, Edmund, Florence, Mass.
Griffin, Maurice E.
Gillis, James
Higgins, Michael J.
Hulten, Emil
Hoskins, Wm. V. Transferred to band.
Hills, Ike T. Promoted to Corporal.
Hiltbrand, Frederick W.
Hotchkiss, Charles R.
Holden, Benedict M., Bristol.
Hubbell, Eugene B., Bristol.
Kagei, Albert
Kane, Cornelius F. (Died Oct. 12th.)
Keith, James L.
Kellerman, Emil
Kennedy, John F.
Kelliher, Simon J. Promoted to Corporal.
Kinderlin, Edward
Kilmurray, Michael J., Hartford.
King, Charles F.
King, John T.
Kennedy, Thomas, Gloversville, N. Y. Transferred to band.
Larson, Gustaf
Lavine, Jacob A.
Lgor, Adolph
Lindquist, Albert
Magner, John J. Promoted to Corporal.
Manning, Edward J. Transferred to band.
Martin, Robert M., Hartford.
Markham, Patrick J.
McCarthy, James
McAvay, John
Merget, Richard V.
McInerny, Matthew
Messenger, Charles
Moody, William
Nelson, Julius
Neurath, Frank A.
O'Mara, Michael
Osterman, Charles A. Promoted to Corporal.
Packard, Joseph, Hartford.
Phelps, Wilbur B.
Prelle, Charles G.
Prevost, Charles F.
Prior, Andrew. (Died Oct. 2d.)
Quinn, Frank W.
Roper, Thomas J.
Rourke, Thomas, Hartford.
Schofield, William T.
Smith, Charles H.
Sperl, Adolph A.
St. Jacques, Lafayette
Sullivan, John
Stayna, Michael
Shea, John F.
Sakelsky, Mike

Tobin, Thomas P.
Wadsworth, Arthur
Walsh, Michael, Southington.
Westover, Frederick H. Promoted to Corporal. (Died Oct. 17th.)
Young, Myron

Company F, of Hartford.

Mustered into the U. S. Service, May 17, 1898.

Captain Charles W. Newton.
1st Lieutenant George W. Ripley, East Hartford.
2d Lieutenant Frank H. Smith.
1st Sergeant William H. Talcott.
Quartermaster-Sergeant Frederick A. Seidler.
Sergeant Herbert G. Bailey.
Sergeant William C. Simmons.
Sergeant Andrew B. Marshall.
Sergeant Herbert A. Wiley.
Corporal Frank M. Jones.
Corporal Frank E. Clark.
Corporal John E. Piddock.
Corporal George D. Robins.
Corporal Sidney W. Ackerman.
Corporal Benjamin C. McKenney.
Musician Thomas W. Foley.
Musician Philip B. Hawk, Middletown.
Artificer Charles H. Finney.
Wagoner Eugene D. Miller.

Privates.

Arnold, Alfred C.
Barton, Jason H., East Hampton.
Beckwith, Julius H., Niantic.
Billings, Fred H.
Belcher, Gregory, New London.
Bonfrey, Bayard C. Promoted to Corporal.
Campbell, John H., New Haven.
Chapman, Morton L.
Carroll, Frank G.
Chase, Nelson L.
Colvocoresses, George M., Litchfield.
Cook, Louis A., New Haven.
Candee, Albert, Harwinton.
Candee, Ralph, Harwinton.
Campbell, Charles L.
Clintsman, William D.
Cornell, Arthur M.
Davidson, Earl E., New Haven. Promoted to Corporal.
Davis, Charles E.
Darling, George O., Bloomfield.
Dixon, Frederick W.. Waterbury.
Douthwaite, Harry W.

Dowen, George J., Burnside.
Dresser, Wilfred H.
Doherty, Charles, Jr.
Embler, Ralph H.
Fisher, Irving L. Promoted to Corporal.
Fletcher, Emerson C.
Flagg, Howard A., West Hartford. Promoted to Corporal.
Green, Harry D.
Greene, Edward C., New Haven.
Gooding, Earl W.
Hale, Arthur H., Rocky Hill.
Hall, George R.
Hawkins, Claude B., Columbia.
Hollingsworth, Harry E.
Holmes, Fred G., East Hartford.
Horton, Thomas
Hutchins, Nelson
Hastings, Walter S.
Howard, Fred G., Florence, Mass.
Hayes, Robert C., St. Johnsbury, Vt.
Joy, Harry E., Deep River.
Kay, George H., Union City.
Lane, Robert.
Lacey, Herbert V. (Discharged May 28th.)
Linsley, Ray K., Suffield.
Lowenhaupt, Ralph
Lincoln, Robert M.
Lyman, Frank W.
Marsh, Frank T.
Martin, Fred M.
Montgomery, Edward L., South Manchester.
Montgomery, Thomas H., South Manchester.
Mountain, John S.
Miller, John
Miller, Robert G., West Hartford.
MacEwen, Hugh C., Jr., Florence, Mass.
McCook, George S.
McVan, John J.
Newman, James F.
Norris, Louis A. (Died Oct. 11th.)
Obryon, Tompkins H.
Owen, Ernest L.
Owen, Hans C.
Pettys, George J.
Pearson, William T.
Parker, Arthur V.
Pickard, Ward W. Promoted to Corporal. (Discharged Sept. 8th.)
Powers, Almond D.
Rich, Alfred T.
Richardson, Ralph R. Promoted to Corporal.
Ross, Herbert A. Promoted to Corporal.
Rice, Sanford A., Florence, Mass.

Reynolds, Forrest H., West Hartford.
Schuler, Louis A.
Sedgwick, Benjamin, Brooklyn, N. Y.
Schuster, Anthony F., Rocky Hill.
Shields, Thomas H., Watertown.
Shortall, Thomas F., Milford, Mass.
Stevens, George T., Guilford. Transferred to Hospital Corps U. S. A., July 18th.
Tabor, Mallery W.
Thomas, Noel D.
Travers, Edward S., Middletown.
Vinton, Louis E., South Windsor.
Walsh, Eugene T.
Wilcox, Harry E.
Woods, James C.
Wilkes, Thomas, Jr.
Wrench, George E.
Yarrow, Ernest A., Middletown.

Company G, of Manchester.

Mustered into the U. S. Service, May 17, 1898.

Captain Joel M. Nichols.
1st Lieutenant J. Davenport Cheney.
2d Lieutenant Lewis J. Doolittle, Hartford.
1st Sergeant Charles O. Lord.
Quartermaster-Sergeant Alfred C. House.
Sergeant Phillip Fraher.
Sergeant Edmund M. Ogden.
Sergeant Gustave H. Leidholdt.
Sergeant Charles B. Warren.
Corporal James E. Sherman.
Corporal Thomas J. Scott.
Corporal Harry Nelson.
Corporal Seth L. Cheney.
Corporal John Connelly, Jr.
Corporal William F. Madden.
Musician William Crawford, Jr.
Musician Michael Spillane.
Artificer Gordon W. Dunn.
Wagoner John J. O'Neill. Hartford.

Privates.

Aveson, Alfred
Anderson, Albert
Aitken, James C.
Barry, Michael F.
Birath, Gustaf
Berggian, Alexander, So. Manchester
Behreud, Joseph J., South Manchester.
Carlson, Charles J.
Clark, Louis E.
Connor, Patrick. Promoted to Corporal.

Chency, Ward. (Discharged to accept commission as Lieut. 4th Inf. U. S. A., July 25th.)
Cuff, Edward C., Hartford.
Carney, John F.
Chamberlain, Austin H.
Colton, Archie W.
Cranick, Charles A., Hartford.
Donnellan, Frank P., Buckland. (Died October 20th.)
Dux, Fred.
Dougan, Robert B.
Doolan, John J.
Dougherty, Charles C., Hartford.
Donahue, Patrick F.
Ethridge, John B.
Fraher, Daniel
Fox, Andrew J.
Flint, Fred C., Hartford.
Finlay, John
Flory, William A., South Manchester.
Falknor, Clark T., Hartford.
Grabofski, Charles H. Promoted to Corporal.
Grabbe, Conrad H.
Garland, Daniel L.
Grogan, Edward, South Manchester.
Harrison, Thomas
Holmquist, Edward
Hultman, Charles J.
Hall, Wm. J.
Johnson, George. Promoted to Corporal.
Keeney, Newton C.
Kerrigan, John J., Hartford.
Keating, Arthur E.
Lahey, John V.
Lee, Samuel F., Bolton.
Lindell, Uno
Lombard, George, Bolton Notch.
McCrea, Mark C., Hartford.
Minke, Charles M.
McCann, John J.
Malkin, Richard L.
Mullonette, Julius
Moynihan, Cornelius
Maxwell, Frank E. Y.
McVeigh, Patrick F., So. Manchester.
Mallon, Wm. J., South Manchester.
McDonald, John E., Hartford.
Mulligan, John, Hartford.
Newberry, Henry G., Buckland. (Discharged Aug. 20th, disability.)
Nichols, Wm. J. Promoted to Corporal.
Norquist, Peter L. Promoted to Corporal.
Nelson, Carl F.
Olcott, Harry E. Promoted to Corporal.
Pohl, Fritz
Popple, Thomas W.

Park, William, Suffield.
Prentice, Wm. J., South Manchester.
Robinson, William
Ritchie, David
Raineault, Leon, Collinsville.
Smith, George J.
Sinnamon, Edwin
Sullivan, Daniel J.
Sullivan, James, Buckland.
Shields, Samuel
Scherwitzsky, Frederick W.
Seastrand, Ernest
Shields, Hugh, South Manchester.
Shields, David, South Manchester.
Smith, Richard, Quarryville.
Silow, Walfrid, Hartford.
Sweeney, Frank, South Manchester.
Sullivan, Timothy, Poquonock.
Taylor, Fred B.
Tennent, Harry F., Hebron. Transferred to band.
Thompson, Joseph
Tripp, Adelbert
Twarz, Richard, Rockville.
Veitch, James R. Transferred to band May 28th.
Waddle, John
Wolski, Thomas, Hartford.
Westland, Alfred, South Manchester.

Company H, of Hartford.

Mustered into the U. S. Service, May 17, 1898.

Captain William E. Mahoney.
1st Lieutenant William A. Sparks.
2d Lieutenant James Smith.
1st Sergeant Patrick J. White.
Sergeant John F. Landrigan. Promoted to Quartermaster-Sergeant.
Sergeant Thomas J. Coyle.
Sergeant Maurice C. Foley.
Sergeant Patrick Callaghan.
Corporal William M. Clark.
Corporal Joseph F. Healey. Promoted to Sergeant.
Corporal John B. Stevens.
Corporal John F. White.
Corporal Phil Ensling, Jr. ·
Musician Charles H. Wittig. Transferred to band.
Musician Elith N. C. Madsen.
Artificer Archibald J. Roulston.
Wagoner Frank A. Linsoth.

Privates.

Adams, Lester J., Windsor Locks.
Adler, Harry S.
Atchison, George

Barton, Seymour B.
Buckley, Jeremiah J.
Baker, Matthew M.
Burns, Wm. H.
Bowen, Edward
Brimble, Ernest W.
Blicher, August W.
Bailey, Philip H., Windsor Locks. Promoted to Corporal.
Bosworth, Charles H.
Clounan, James H.
Cunningham, Thomas H.
Cowles, Royal M.
Clark, Julius W., Bristol.
Carroll, Michael
Conner, John F.
Cooper, Wm. H.
Duffy, Michael J.
Duffy, Joseph P.
Duffy, Thomas F.
Driesnack, Albert M. Transferred to band.
Donahue, Thomas J., Jr.
Ellison, James
Furlong, Thomas V.
Fogarty, Cornelius J.
Golden, Peter J.
Gastonguay, Joseph G.
Gourley, Fred F., Windsor Locks.
Harper, Joseph P.
Hawkins, Wallace V.
Herron, Robert
Hebron, Robert F.
Hines, James J.
Hedberg, Charles V.
Hoban, John J.
Hines, John B.
Hines, James M.
Horan, Francis. Promoted to Corporal.
Johnson. Hugh M.
Jones, Sala D., Middletown. Transferred to band.
King, George, Jr.
Kelleher, William. Promoted to Corporal.
Keena, Michael T. Promoted to Corporal.
Kearns, James F., Jr., Burnside.
Lohs, Fred W.
Lyons, Philip
Low, Wm. B., Jr.
Lewis, Fred H.
Lewis, Howard C.
Loveland, Edward E., Seneca Falls, N. Y.
Mack, Herbert D. Appointed Musician.
Mahoney, Wm. H.
Marenholtz, Fred T.
McCue, Thomas J.
McCarthy, Dennis F. Promoted to Corporal.

McMahon, Henry P.
McDonough, James P.
McPherson, John
McKee, James F.
Mooney, James P.
Mullen, Thomas F., Jr.
Murphy, Edward T.
Mottram, Alfred
Munro, Kenneth McK.
Murphy, Thomas E.
Murphy, Michael D., So. Glastonbury.
McGregor, John B.
McGinn, Edward J.
Manahan, Thomas F., Windsor Locks.
Manion, Edward J.
O'Flaherty, John P.
Reeve, Wm. R.
Reese, Wm. E.
Readel, Wm. H.
Raisbeck, Bertie John, Suffield.
Raisbeck, Ralph, Suffield.
Shields, Howard L.
Sheedy, Thomas F.
Selleck, Edwin H.
Van Buren, Henry S.
Walsh, Daniel. Promoted to Corporal.
Welch, Wm. J.
Wilcox, Robert. Promoted to Corporal.
Watson, Wm. T.
Watson, Alexander
Wucherer, Julius
Woodworth, Walter G.
Wittig, Louis H. Promoted to Corporal.
Wadstrum, Justus
White, Richard

Company I, of New Britain.

Mustered into the U. S. Service, May 17, 1898.

Captain Charles H. Moore.
1st Lieutenant William J. Rawlings.
2d Lieutenant Samuel E. Magson.
1st Sergeant Jesse J. Broadbent.
Quartermaster-Sergeant Ventres A. Clark.
Sergeant Frank D. Clark.
Sergeant Alfred H. Griswold.
Sergeant Claude D. Clark.
Sergeant Patrick Crowe.
Corporal Harry E. Smith.
Corporal Edward J. McBriarty.
Corporal James P. McNeil.
Corporal Reinhold Schell.
Corporal Willard J. Dyson.
Corporal Chester L. Wyman, Waterbury.
Musician John H. Mils, Hartford.

Musician Walter J. Hawthorne.
Artificer Albert E. Lane, Hartford.
    Promoted to Corporal.
Wagoner Lewis T. Bacon.

Privates.

Anderson, August
Boquist, Martin
Brown, Frank
Burns, James J.
Carlson, Gustaf A.
Carroll, Dennis A.
Cheney, George Y. C. Promoted to Corporal.
Chute, Wm. F., Jr. (Died Sept. 3d.)
Conley, Eugene
Cooney, John L.
Carlson, Carl E.
Coffey, James F.
Damon, Herbert H., Berlin.
Dunbar, John A.
Dunn, Daniel J., Hartford.
Dyson, William
Eagan, Thomas F.
Fields, Allie D., South Glastonbury.
Fitzgerald, Peter, Hartford.
Flint, Edwin H., South Glastonbury.
Genter, Charles
Gilligan, Wm. P.
Guenther, Rudolph F.
Goodwin, Frank D.
Hansen, Hans, Hartford.
Hultar, Emil. Transferred to Co. E July 6th.
Hayes, Robert L. Promoted to Artificer.
Hebb, Morris. Promoted to Corporal.
Herriander, Fred
Hunt, Henry H., So. Glastonbury.
Hallen, Andrew F.
Hawthorn, Walter J.
Hughes, John J., Hartford.
Joyce, Michael P., Terryville.
Joyce, David F., Holyoke, Mass
Johnson, Charles
Kelley, Thomas
Kalik, Micke
Kienell, Fred .C.
Kiernan, William
Keefer, Charles C., Bridgeport.
Kilkelly, Thomas F., Holyoke, Mass.
Koop, Ernest H. G.
Larson, John
Larson, Axel
Larson, Charles O.
Larson, Christie, Hartford.
Lehman, Frederick
Leidholdt, Henry F., Manchester.
Lind, Alvin
Lutostauski, Peter

Lutz, John
Mack, John. (Deserted Sept. 15th.)
Magson, Joe S., Brooklyn, N. Y.
Mahon, Joseph, East Hartford.
Mayer, Joseph, Hartford.
Merrill, Charles O., Hartford.
McCabe, James, Berlin.
Mulligan, James H. Discharged for disability Sept. 12th.
McGrath, Frank F. Promoted to Corporal.
Mix, Daniel
McCollum, Oleon, Hartford.
Nielson, Henry, Hartford.
Nord, Charles, Hartford.
Orton, Oliver. (Died Oct. 28th.)
Pearson, Adolph, Hartford.
Peterson, Alfred K., Hartford.
Peterson, Andrew, Hartford.
Pierson, Wilbur B., Hartford.
Prendergast, James
Richter, Gunther
Riley, Patrick J.
Reid, Matthew L., Hartford.
Rosengren, John, Hartford.
Ryberg, Gottfried, Hartford.
Ryquist, Per J. Promoted to Corporal.
Samlow, William F.
Sheehan, John J.
Sperry, Eugene
Sproch, Andro
Stevens, John E.
Sullivan, Eugene, East Hartford.
Sullivan, John R.
Towers, Samuel E.
Tryon, George W., Kensington.
Veinovitch, Aimen
Wells, Edwin
Wilcox, Arthur H., Berlin. Promoted to Corporal.
Williams, George, Hartford.
Wylie, Joseph, Windsor.
Zwirz, William, Hartford.

Company K, of Hartford.

Mustered into the U. S. Service, May 17, 1898.

Captain Henry H. Saunders.
1st Lieutenant Edward H. Waterman.
2d Lieutenant Nathaniel G. Valentine.
1st Sergeant Samuel G. Huntington.
Quartermaster-Sergeant Robert L. Beebe.
Sergeant Richard W. DeLamater.
Sergeant Henry L. Huntington.
Sergeant Henry T. Holt.
Sergeant John D. Bonaface.
Corporal Charles A. Carroll.
Corporal Francis M. Johnson.
Corporal Louis Silvernail.
Corporal Cyrus E. Wheeler.
Corporal George K. Dwyer.
Corporal Ralph B. Pierce.
Musician Robert R. Ashwell.
Musician Henry P. Camp.
Wagoner Edward F. Ahern.
Artificer Guy F. Rowland.

Privates.

Appleton, Frederick L. Promoted to Corporal.
Barber, Wm. R.
Barker, Alfred
Bassett, Merton W.
Barrows, Charles D.
Bryant, Harry E.
Brigham, William E.
Brown, William H.
Burwell, Francis C.
Borland, Henry L.
Beauchamp, George G.
Brown, Dwight E., Simsbury.
Burwell, Joseph
Cannon, Archie L.
Cadwell, Frank J.
Case, Robert A.
Campbell, Wm. F. Promoted to Corporal.
Case, William O.
Chamberlain, Henry H.
Converse, Lawrence A.
Clapp, Howard S.
Denison, Frank E.
Denison, Frederick R.
Denniston, Minott C.
Dickinson, Howard L.
Dimock, Irving. (Died Sept. 21st.)
Driscoll, Clarence J.
Eno, John E.
Fisher, Alfred M.
Fulton, Albert C.
Fuller, Frank E.
Fowler, Edward C., Bloomfield.
Gale, Charles D., New York city. (Died Oct. 7th.)
Gillette, Henry C.
Gruener, Theodore. Promoted to Corporal.
Hall, Henry H.
Hatton, William H.
Hynes, James P.
Hayden, Edgar G.
Henderson, James D.
Hollis, Eben C.
Humphrey, Robert M.
Judson, Edward W.
Johnson, William C.
Kirkley, Robert
Knox, John B., Jr.
Kober, Edward G.
Low, William W. Promoted to Corporal.
Landerman, Myer

Marion, Otis D.
Marvel, Eugene T.
Malloy, Peter J.
McGrath, Michael E.
McKone, John J.
McKee, Robert A.
Morley, Reuben H. Transferred to 32d Mich. V. I., June 13th.
Morgan, Joseph
Morgan, Jeremiah
Moran, James L.
McLaughlin, James
Numan, Edward P.
Oviatt, Edward M.
Pattison, George E.
Perry, John B., West Haven.
Pierce, Charles W. Transferred to band.
Pierce, Martin A., Rainbow. (Died Sept. 27th.)
Potter, James H.
Prescott, Albert N. Mustered with N. C. Staff as Commissary-Sergeant.
Pimm, Alfred B.
Rathbun, Edward H.
Roberts, William A.
Root, Herbert E.
Ripley, Herbert J.
Rogers, William H.
Sanderson, Edward F. Promoted to Corporal.
Sandner, Anthony J., West Haven.
Sarvan, Frank H.
Scharper, Ernest A.
Schults, Carl H.
Shea, Maurice B.
Sobieralski, John A.
Sherman, Frederick L., West Haven.
Thayer, George B.
Tinkham, Charles A.
Thompson, Michael J.
Vibert, Robert K.
Ward, Edward M. Promoted to Corporal.
Walsh, Thomas H.
Webster, Roy C.
Wheelock, Paul L.
Wolcott, Charles B.
Wiley, Royal H.
Zoller, Arthur W., West Haven. (Died Oct. 18th.)

Company L, of Meriden.

Recruited after Regiment was mustered. Mustered into the ·U. S. Service, July 9, 1898.

Captain Charles B. Bowen.
1st Lieutenant Delbert R. Jones.
2d Lieutenant Raymond G. Keeney, Somersville.

1st Sergeant Philip T. Vibert.
Quartermaster-Sergeant Arthur A. Abel.
Sergeant William H. Rees.
Sergeant Howard H. Bartram.
Sergeant Walter L. Bevins.
Sergeant William H. Banner.
Corporal Clifford A. Hauschild.
Corporal Charles E. Wachtelhauser.
Corporal Fred H. Relyea.
Corporal Frederick C. Benziger, Yalesville. Reduced to the ranks Sept. 1, 1898.
Corporal Thomas P. Timothy, Wallingford.
Corporal Othniel Ives.
Musician Joseph G. Aichler.
Musician Edwin F. Bolton, Wallingford.
Artificer Eugene W. Early.
Wagoner Louis E. Coutermash.

Privates.

Abel, Alfred A., Hartford. Discharged Aug. 11th, disability.
Ammann, Louis
Anthony, George H., Southington.
Benson, Axel M.
Bickford, Louis H.
Borchard, Ferdinand L.
Bofird, Maxwell
Bower, Clarence A., Yalesville.
Brechlin, Charles A.
Burdett, Charles S.
Burr, Albert A. Promoted to Corporal.
Burr, Walter W.
Carlin, Philip T.
Carter, Edward
Collins, James F.
Conraux, Anton. Transferred to band.
Cooper, Arthur
Cox. John J., Wallingford.
Cobb, Rollo W., South Meriden.
Dainton, Frank E.
Dulicke, Frank A.
Dupree, Charles J.
Durkin, Frank W., Bristol.
Dussault, Alfred.
Fletcher, John W., New Haven.
Folce, Henry E.
Foran, John V.
Francis, John J., Wallingford.
Galvin, Thomas
Gardner, Willis W.
Goldstein, Louis
Gollnick, Fred
Goodman, Michael J.
Gracey, Joseph H.
Granger, Harry C.
Hiller, Wm. G.

Harvey, Harry E.
Hennessy, Maurice
Hickey, John W.   Promoted to Corporal.
Higgins, Edward
Hogan, Edward T.
Hopwood, John
Hourigan, James D.
Hyde, William G.
Jirma, Michael, Wallingford.
Kaschube, Herman
Kay, John
Kelly, John J.
Kennedy, John J., Wallingford.
King, John
King, Joseph R.   Promoted to Corporal.
Kline, Charles J.
Knoblauch, Wm. J.
Kline, August O.
Lee, Wm. D.
Lacoursiere, Philip F. F.
Lenihan, James J.
Lucchini, Arthur C.   (Died Oct. 20th.)
McGoldrick, John F.
McLaughlin, Edward T.
Mulroney, Patrick J.
Noonan, Wm. E.
Numann, August
O'Donnell, Charles J.
Olson, Charles A.
Penfield, Wm. L.   Promoted to Corporal.
Pickhardt, Frank W.
Plunkett, John F.
Perkins, Charles S., Jr.   Promoted to Corporal.
Reama, Walter S.
Rogers, Eugene C.
Royce, Walter H., Bristol.
Runge, Julius G.
Russell, Lorenzo C.
Senecal, Joseph
Shea, George W.   Promoted to Corporal.
Shea, Patrick J., Norwich.   Transferred from Co. A 3d.
Sheehey, Anthony A., Wallingford.
Shinkey, John J.
Shortell, Patrick J.
Siegel, Herbert J.
Skinner, Leonard.   Promoted to Corporal.
Smith, Michael
Stanley, Harry.   Discharged Aug. 16th for disability.
Stillman, Floyd W.
Tighe, Thomas E.
Todd, Whitney A., Yalesville.
Walsh, Michael

Wollschlager, Frank M.
Wren, William, Middletown.
Young, William G.

Company M, of Danbury.

(*Formerly Co. G, 4th Regt. C. N. G.*).
Mustered into the U. S. Service, July 14, 1898.

Captain Vincent M. King.
1st Lieutenant Charles Lord.
2d Lieutenant Cyrus E. Ryder.
1st Sergeant Emil W. Ericson.
Quartermaster-Sergeant Emil A. Ihloff.
Sergeant George Nelson.
Sergeant Benjamin H. Turner.
Sergeant Orlando C. Kent.
Sergeant Wilbur L. Pike.
Corporal John C. Woolard.
Corporal Charles L. Walters.
Corporal Oscar E. Parks.
Corporal George W. Hitchcock.
Corporal Alfred Heim.
Corporal Walter F. Nichols.
Corporal Charles H. Miller.
Corporal Robert W. Menzies.
Corporal Leonard E. Smith.
Corporal Charles Avery.
Corporal Frank W. Stone.
Corporal Martin C. Braun.
Musician John L. Quinn.
Musician Fred A. Claus.
Artificer James Donovan.
Wagoner John Kroha.

Privates.

Abbott, Charles
Barrett, Richard M.
Barnum, Howard S.
Barber, Edward
Bloom, Emil
Brotherton, Bennett L.
Brownell, Charles H.
Butler, Guy H.
Carson, Samuel, Bethel.
Clark, Daniel J.
Clemons, John H., New York city.
Cosgrove, John J.
Cole, Frank S., Bethel.
Currid, Lawrence
Davis, George F.
Dorgan, Dennis F., Redding.
Durbin, Charles B.
Erwin, Gay, New Milford.
Ferguson, Ernest
Fitzpatrick, James H., Bethel.
Finnegan, Christopher B.

Ginty, James
Gilmartin, Charles, Bethel.
Himple, Samuel, Bethel
Hunt, Dominic W., Bethel.
Horton, Edward D.
Hornig, August G.
Hopkins, Aba J., Bethel.
Horton, Wesley D.
Hull, Charles
Hueston, Charles W.
Joyce, Howard B., Bethel.
Kernick, Albert, Bethel.
Kenny, Michael, Bethel.
Kroha, Edward C.
Larson, Charles J., Bethel.
Lynch, James L.
Lyons, Herbert C.
Magersuppe, Henry
McMahon, Martin J.
McFarland, Frank P.
McNamara, Michael J.
McManus, Matthew L., Bethel.
McNamara, John
McLaughlin, Michael J.
Miller, David A.
Morahan, William, Hartford.
Montgomery, Wm. H.
Murphy, Frank
Morgan, William, Bethel.
Nevins, William
Norman, William, Southbury.
Norman, Frank J., Southbury.

Oakley, Charles H.
Oakley, George E.
Odell, Odie
Odell, Lester
Osborne, Wm. H.
O'Sullivan, Thomas F.
Pardee, Fred C.
Pawlowski, Antone
Peavey, Thomas
Pelletier, Louis
Prout, William L.
Purdy, Albert J.
Purdy, Hart A.
Purdy, William A.
Quinn, Thomas. Transferred to band.
Quinn, Martin
Reagan, Michael, Bethel.
Reagan, Peter, Bethel.
Rosso, John R.
Ryan, Michael, Bethel.
Ryan, Frank X., Bethel.
Sullivan, James J.
Taylor, Howard J.
Teller, Stephen, Bethel.
Torrance, William M.
Warburton, Irving, Bethel.
Wakem, Paul S.
Wheeler, Frank F.
Wood, Robert E.
Woodin, Nelson H.
Young, Charles R.

First Regiment Volunteer Artillery.

Battery A, Light, of Branford.

Mustered into the U. S. Service, Niantic, May 19, 1898. Mustered out, Oct. 25, 1898, New Haven.

Captain Barlow S. Honce.
1st Lieutenant William J. O'Brien.
1st Lieutenant Herbert T. Weston, New Haven.
2d Lieutenant John F. Kinney.
2d Lieutenant James A. Honce, Guilford.
1st Sergeant John W. Lynch.
Quartermaster-Sergeant Edward B. Treat, New Haven.
Veterinary Sergeant, William S. Clancey.
Sergeant Frank V. Chappell, New London.
Sergeant Thomas G. Fisher.
Sergeant William D. Massey.

Sergeant Alton Spencer, Guilford.
Sergeant David C. Twichell, Hartford. Discharged Oct. 8th to accept appointment as 2d Lieutenant Co. F, 3d C. V. I.; 1st Lieutenant and Adjutant Nov. 4th.
Sergeant Frank M. White, Guilford.
Corporal Charles J. Anderson, Guilford.
Corporal John W. Baisley.
Corporal John S. Dailey, Guilford.
Corporal Oliver I. Griswold, Guilford.
Corporal Carleton C. Jones, New Haven.
Corporal Patrick McGuire.
Corporal John J. Massey.
Corporal Robert A. Oughton, Guilford.
John R. Paxton, Jr., New Haven.
Peter W. Plass, Guilford.
Corporal Harleigh Parkhurst, New Haven.
Corporal Charles L. Sherwood, Southport.

Corporal George F. Sanford, New Haven. Discharged Oct. 8th to accept appointment as 2d Lieutenant, Co. E, 3d C. V. I.
Corporal Charles M. Tilley.
Corporal George C. Walsh.
Farrier Frank B. Aninger, Hartford.
Farrier Horace L. Carter, Hartford.
Artificer Stephen H. White, Guilford.
Artificer Harry E. Rogers.
Saddler William N. Vaile, New Haven. Removed and made private May 19th.
Musician William H. Hotchkiss, Guilford.
Musician James E. Mathews.
Wagoner Henry Hill, Guilford.

Privates.

Ahern, John
Anderson, Elmer J., Guilford.
Barton, George L., Norwich.
Barnes, Charles C., Guilford.
Bangs, Merwin B., New Haven.
Barnett, Wm. L., New Haven.
Beach, Sidney, Branford. (Died Sept. 28th.)
Beecher, Norman B., New Haven.
Bell, Archibald M., New Haven. Discharged for disability Aug. 23d.
Benner, Burnham C., New Haven.
Born, Frank J., New Haven.
Buist, George L., Jr., New Haven. Transferred to Hospital Corps Aug. 31st.
Bennett, Clarence O., Norwich.
Birge, Nathan R., Bristol.
Bissell, Arthur H., Montclair, N. J.
Bogart, John D., New Haven.
Bohan, Michael T., New Haven.
Callahan, Eugene
Chaipel, Clifford L.
Chappell, Alfred S., New London.
Cheney, Austin, New Haven.
Clish, Harry, Norwich. Promoted to Saddler.
Cowdrey, Nathaniel H., New Haven.
Cruise, Richard, Guilford.
Cumings, Ralph H., New Haven.
Calhoun, Charles M., Springfield, Mass.
Callahan, Joseph H., New Haven.
Chapman, Grenville T., Springfield, Mass.
Cowan, Samuel M., Waterbury.
Deegan, John
Dwyer, Michael F., Ansonia.
de Forest, Lee, New Haven.
Doolittle, Warren J., Mt. Carmel.
Downey, Wm. J., New Haven.
Egan, Charles E., Waterbury.
Egan, John J., New Haven.

Fowler, Henry B., Guilford.
Fuller, Frederick, Guilford.
Feeter, George I., Little Falls, N. Y.
Florence, Charles E., New Haven.
Gause, Frederick T., New Haven. Discharged Aug. 26th.
Greiner, Oscar H., Meriden. Discharged for disability Aug. 5th.
Gilmore, Wm. B., Guilford.
Gearns, Edward S., New Haven.
Gullans, Erik
Graham, Frank L., New Haven.
Granger, Charles E., Waterbury.
Guerin, Harold C., New Haven.
Griffin, James L., New Haven.
Greenberg, Michell G., New Haven.
Harrison, Claud R., Guilford.
Holden, Francis P., Meriden.
Honce, Charles A., Guilford.
How, Louis, New Haven.
Howard, James L., Jr., Hartford.
Hubbell, Wm. S., Jr., New Haven.
Hutchins, Wm. H., New Haven.
Kelly, Wm. H., Norwich.
Kniffin, Arthur H.
Kniffin, Clifford E.
Kirkham, Charles M., Springfield, Mass.
Killoy, John E., New Haven.
Ledyard, Augustus C., New Haven. Discharged to accept appointment as 2d Lieutenant 2d U. S. I.
Luiskey, Nicholas, Guilford. Discharged for disability Aug. 5th.
Lloyd, Charles R., Jr., New Haven, Discharged to accept appointment as 2d Lieutenant 6th U. S. Art., Bat. I.
Loeb, Arthur S., New Haven.
Luis, Frank, New Haven.
Lyman, George E., New Haven.
MacLane, Paul B., New Haven.
MacMillin, Marion M., New Haven. Discharged to accept appointment as Captain and Asst. Q.-M., U. S. V., July 23d.
Mannix, Dennis
Marshall, Edward E., New Haven.
Marshall, Samuel A., New Haven.
McCarthy, Timothy J.
McGrail, Eugene J.
McNamara, John T., New Haven.
Mooney, Luke F., Guilford.
Moore, George C., New Haven.
Moran, John, Guilford. Discharged for disability Aug. 23d.
Murdock, Wm. M., New Haven.
Murphy, William, Guilford.
Mansfield, Thomas E., New Haven.
Miller, Charles H., Waterbury.
Marlow, John H., New Haven.
Marlow, Wm. F., Fair Haven.

18

Marks, Wm. E., Waterbury.
Maroney, Wm. A., New Haven.
McCabe, John H., New Haven.
McGovern, Frank J., New Haven.
McMahon, Thomas, Shelton.
Moran, George F., New Haven.
Neef, Joseph A., Waterbury.
Noonan, William F., New Haven.
O'Brien, Frank A., New Haven.
O'Hara, Thomas F., New Haven.
Packer, Wm. S., Jr., New Haven.
Page, Charles H.
Parker, Charles V., New Haven.
Parmelee, Cleon A., New Haven.
Rafter, Edward A., New Haven.
Reynolds, John J., New Haven.
Reynolds, John T.
Ricketts, Joseph J., New Haven.
Ripley, Julien A.
Rockwell, Maxwell W., New Haven.
Rodden, Bernie
Roberts, George, New Haven.
Roesler, Edward, New Haven.
Rourke, Michael H.
Selin, Edward
Seymour, John B., New Haven.
Scanlan, Michael A.
Shea, John T.
Shroder, Wm. J., New Haven.
Slocovich, Wm. P., New Haven.
Spencer, Frederick J., Guilford.
Spencer, George W., Guilford.
Stannard, Frederick, Guilford.
Strobel, Fritz
Suiter, Charles E., New Haven.
Sullivan, Daniel J., Guilford.
Steele, Wm. S., Torrington. Discharged
to accept appointment as 2d Lieuten-
ant Co. D, 3d Regt, Sept. 12th; 1st
Lieutenant, Jan. 31, 1899.
Sweet, Joseph, Guilford.
Sykes, Walter H., Jr., New Haven.
Taylor, Charlie, Guilford.
Thrall, George C., New Haven.
Thompson, Clarence S., New Haven.
Tichborne, Walter F. C., New Haven.
Treat, Frank L., Wallingford.
Trowbridge, Cecil H., Milford.
Tuckerman, Julius, New Haven.
Walsh, Thomas F.
Watts, John M., New Haven.
Wildman, Frederick J., Guilford.
Wright, James T., Guilford.
Wilcox, John W., Putnam.
White, Thaddeus C., Middletown.
Winslow, Wm. A., New Haven.
Worrall, Walter L., New Haven. Dis-
charged Sept. 14th.
Wedge, Charlie. Guilford. Discharged
Aug. 5th for disability.

Battery B, of Bridgeport.

(Formerly Co. K, 4th Regt. C. N. G. Mustered into the U. S. Service, May 19, 1898. Mustered out, Dec. 20, 1898, Bridgeport.

Captain Fred J. Breckbill.
1st Lieutenant John A. Leonard.
2d Lieutenant Wm. A. Evans.
2d Lieutenant Wm. Baseley, New London.
1st Sergeant Joseph W. Smith. Mustered out Oct. 27th, order Secy. of War.
Sergeant Charles F. Gushee. Discharged Nov. 2d.
Sergeant Richard C. Smith. Reduced to ranks at own request May 31st.
Sergeant Charles Andres.
Sergeant Horace W. Pigg, Jr.
Sergeant Frederick W. Teele. Promoted to 1st Sergeant.
Sergeant George T. Eadie.
Sergeant Joseph Havey. Reduced at own request July 1, 1898.
Sergeant Alexander Weed, Jr., Stamford.
Sergeant Walter Smith, Danbury.
Sergeant Henry B. Phillips.
Sergeant Philip Powers.
Sergeant George Straight. Reduced to ranks; mustered out Oct. 27th.
Sergeant Edmond E. Monahan.
Sergeant Thomas J. Lyons.
Sergeant John Walker, Danbury.
Sergeant Anson D. Barnes.
Sergeant Wm. M. Skinner.
Sergeant Robert B. Auld. Reduced to ranks July 20, 1898.
Sergeant George F. Gammons, West Haven.
Sergeant Ernest P. Leonard.
Sergeant Charles F. Starr, Danbury. Reduced to ranks; mustered out Oct. 27th.
Sergeant Wm. S. Coughlin.
Corporal Arthur E. Chase. Promoted to Sergeant.
Corporal Harry W. Fuller. Mustered out Oct. 27th.
Corporal Edward S. Davis, Danbury.
Corporal Thomas J. Gore.
Corporal Wm. C. Allen. Reduced to ranks July 23d.
Corporal Herbert J. Reilly. Promoted to Sergeant.
Corporal Herbert Leid, Danbury.
Corporal James A. McDonald.

Corporal Francis E. Hoyt. Reduced to ranks July 20th, order dept. of East.

Corporal Charles A. Barnes, Stamford.

Musician John Raycroft. Reduced to ranks; mustered out Oct. 27th.

Musician Wm. H. Langlan. Reduced to ranks; mustered out Oct. 27th.

Artificer Louis J. Herrmann. Promoted to Sergeant.

Artificer Schuyler Hamrick. Reduced to ranks; mustered out Oct. 27th.

Wagoner Martin V. See, So. Norwalk.

Privates.

Alvord, Fred, Stratford.
Alexander, Frank
Alexander, James
Allan, James
Ashton, John T.
Anderson, Charles
Abercrombie, Robert
Adlard, James, South Wilton
Allen, Wm. C.
Bolt, Jerome L.
Buttery, Fred. Discharged July 30th, disability.
Breton, Joseph W., Torrington.
Buck, Charles O., Stratford.
Bardwell, George W. Mustered out, Oct. 27th.
Barwick, John
Burton, Edward. Mustered out Oct. 27th.
Brophy, Joseph. Mustered out Oct. 27th.
Botwright, George
Buckingham, Albert A., Danbury. Promoted to Corporal.
Bowron, Frank J.
Brown, Robert E.
Baker, Frederick
Bell, William, So. Wilton.
Branigan, James
Baldwin, Albert E., So. Norwalk.
Blakeslee, Charles W., Stratford.
Clancy, Patrick
Connor, Charles E.
Curtis, Howard A.
Callahan, John H.
Connor, Walter J.
Clancy, James J. Mustered out Oct. 27th.
Cullen, John U.
Christensen, Charles R. Mustered out Oct. 27th, order Secy. of War.
Connors, John
Cleary, Thomas F.
Cleary, James
Callan, John
Cavenagh, Willis L., Norwalk.

Cannon, John F.
Demery, Albert V. Mustered out Oct. 27th.
Dickinson, Charles P. Promoted to Corporal Oct. 4th.
Deitz, Cassius E. Promoted to Sergeant. Mustered out Oct. 27th.
Donovan, John W.
Danick, Andrew
Dieringer, George W. Appointed musician; discharged Oct. 27th.
Dawson, James L., Derby.
Dobson, George K., Danbury.
Downs, Charles E.
Ennis, James F.
Feely, James E.
Fitzgerald, Richard, South Norwalk.
Furburshaw, John
Fischer, Hugo
Faulkner, James A. Mustered out Oct. 27th.
Flanagan, John P. Promoted to Sergeant July 11th.
Fotch, Charles W.
Godfrey, Howard N., Norwalk. Promoted to Sergeant.
Gerner, Frederick
Gleason, Michael J.
Guarnieri, Charles F., Norwalk.
Ghiotto, Anthony B., South Norwalk.
Garrish, Henry
Gilmore, Wm. G., Norwalk.
Heaply, George E.
Hennesy, William
Hutchinson, Ernest
Henwood, Samuel J., Bethel.
Harrington, Frank, New York city.
Hodge, George E., Danbury.
Healy, George E.
Hanson, John
Hines, Frank
Ives, Fred O.
Judson, Howard, Stratford.
Judson, Henry, Stratford.
Judd, Ernest H.
Keenan, Frederick. Deserted July 8th.
Kilkenny, John. Mustered out Oct. 27th.
Keniston, Charles E.
Keefer, Philip S.
Knapp, Albert E.
Kernan, Charles
Keating, Edward
Letcher, Joseph H.
Lahey, Daniel J., Danbury.
Lowe, Howard E., Danbury.
Lynch, Robert F.
Lawler, James
Leppert, Charles, So. Norwalk.
Moore, Herbert L.
Murphy, Wm. H.
Muth, William H.

Moody, Lester
McCabe, Edward
McClure, Henry
Monaghan, Joseph. Mustered out Oct. 27th.
Murphy, James
Murphy, Michael J.
Moss, Ernest J.
Myers, William A. Mustered out Oct. 27th.
McIntyre, Frederick W.
Murray, Wm. H.
Munson, Hiram
Murray, Charles J.
McCauley, Charles C.
Murtagle, Thomas
McKenna, Jeremiah, New London
Muller, Max W., New Britain.
Makara, Edward J.
McDonald, Michael
Nelson, George
Nichols, Andrew E.
Nichols, Herbert F.
O'Connor, Maurice
O'Connell, John J.
Ogden, James W. Promoted to Artificer. Discharged at Fort Griswold, order Secy. of War, Aug. 31st.
Post, Arthur
Polley, Henry S., Danbury.
Phalen, Patrick J. Discharged for disability July 30, Ft. Griswold.
Ponshow, Julius E. Promoted to Artificer.
Quigley, John
Regnery, Peter
Regnery, Frank W.
Rickel, George
Rooney, Thomas W.
Radcliff, John
Rahm, Oscar, Cleveland, O.
Reilly, Wm.
Rauscher, Fred.
Ramsey, James
Randall, Ernest C. Mustered out Oct. 27th, order Secy. of War.
Rogers, Thomas. Mustered out Oct. 27th, order Secy. of War.
Roberts, Charles F. Transferred to Hospital Corps U. S. A., July 1st.
Stagg, Harry L.
Storck, Matthias
Steele, Wilbur T.
Smith, Daniel C., Milford.
Sheehan, John T.
Spall, Edward C., Stratford.
Schneider, George L.
Smith, Edward M., Middletown.
Smith, Richard C.
Stebbins, Joseph B., Hartford. Appointed musician.

Sanger, Geo. B. Promoted to Artificer.
Sherwood, Harold
Sebas, George J., Jr.
Sullivan, Patrick
Schroh, Jacob
Stenger, Anthony, So. Norwalk.
Smith, Benjamin
Schwarzenberg, Bernhard
Sleight, Harry
Shields, Wm. E. Mustered out Oct. 27th, order Secy. of War.
Smith, James J. Mustered out Oct. 27th, order Secy. of War.
Strickland, Wm. A. Promoted to Corporal.
Taylor, James H.
Thompson, Albert. Promoted to Corporal.
Thibideau, Frederick J.
Tompkins, Samuel
Tate, John
Van Dutton, Alfred H.
Vail, Everett
White, Anthony S.
Wolff, Charles H.
Waite, Walter E.
Wilcox, Howard. Promoted to Corporal.

Battery C, of New Haven.

Recruited at New Haven.

Mustered into the U. S. Service, May 19, 1898. Mustered out, Oct. 31, 1898, New Haven.

Captain Francis G. Beach. Mustered out Oct. 10th, to accept com. as Captain of Co. H, 3d Regiment, C. V. I.
1st Lieutenant Allan M. Osborn. (Died Oct. 1, 1898.)
2d Lieutenant Giles Bishop, Jr., New London. Promoted to Captain.
2d Lieutenant Henry S. Terrell, Winsted. Promoted to 1st Lieutenant.
1st Sergeant Walter G. Penfield. Promoted to 2d Lieutenant
Sergeant Oliver A. Phelps, Wallingford. Promoted to 2d Lieutenant.
Sergeant Frank Corves.
Sergeant James A. Howarth, Jr.
Sergeant Vincent Pasetsk, Wallingford.
Sergeant Michael G. Hoey.
Sergeant Richard J. W. Emery, Torrington.
Sergeant Hans Gronow, Winsted.
Sergeant Edward B. Eames.
Sergeant Franklin W. Allis, Wallingford.

Sergeant George A. Hegeman.
Sergeant Charles N. Burdick, New London.
Sergeant Fred'k W. Schultz, Winsted.
Sergeant James A. Gorman.
Sergeant Peter P. Contois, Westfield.
Sergeant James H. Flaherty. (Died Oct. 9, 1898.)
Sergeant William Noonan.
Sergeant Robert E. Broatch, Middletown.
Sergeant Wm. P. Gilligan, Meriden.
Corporal Harry A. Goodale, New London.
Corporal Lester E. Ferris, Stamford.
Corporal Harry M. Cooke.
Corporal Newton F. Lewis.
Corporal Royal E. Penny, Southport.
Corporal Arthur E. Foley, Winsted.
Corporal Michael R. Clark. Reduced to ranks July 21st. Deserted July 25th.
Corporal Burton M. Welch.
Artificer Charles O'Keeffe.
Artificer George A. Hull.
Musician Frank W. Reed.
Musician Wilbur H. Bradford, Winsted.
Wagoner Charles Jahuke, New York.

Privates.

Adams, John H.
Ball, Charles B.
Bauer, George W.
Bess, Charles, Wallingford.
Beyer, Louis A.
Blieske, Henry C. Deserted Aug. 12th.
Brown, Richard J.
Brown, Wm. J.
Brundage, George A.
Burgess, Frederick L., Torrington.
Burton, Archibald A., Torrington.
Barrett, James J.
Beach, Alburton C., Meriden.
Beardsley, Wm. H.
Brennan, Samuel A.
Bromm, Andrew
Buckingham, Wm. E.
Buckley, Daniel M.
Cadwell, Edward H.
Cahn, Louis W.
Campbell, Walter S., Lanesville.
Casey, Edward J.
Casey, James J.
Casey, Wm. H.
Clement, George
Condon, Wm. J.
Corcoran, James H.
Cremin, Dennis J.
Cuddy, John J.
Cullinan, Stephen W.
Chapman, Harold R.

Clancy, John J.
Coniskey, Wm. J.
Cross, Joseph, Meriden.
Cummings, John J.
Cummings, James N.
Deery, John C.
Dehmer, Joseph J.
Dole, Everett C.
Donnelly, George H.
Donnelly, John J., 1st.
Donnelly, John J., 2d.
Donnelly, Thomas A.
Daily, Martin F.
Duffy, Harry
Dunlay, Charles P.
Deskin, Martin J.
Edwards, Arthur L.
Faith, Leonard P., Meriden.
Finn, James L.
Forsyth, James M. (Died Oct. 13th.)
Funk, Edward H. Discharged for insanity Sept. 23d.
Ferris, James
Farren, Comfort S.
Fitzgerald, John T.
Flood, Wm. J. D.
Foster, John H.
Fuchko, John, Meriden.
Gahan, James
Gilligan, Dennis
Gillon, Thomas H.
Galligan, Andrew
Gasser, Albert
Grady, Harry P., Winsted.
Hackett, Thomas
Hannon, John J.
Harrison, Michael R.
Havens, Eugene B., Meriden.
Hayes, John T., Winsted.
Healy, Michael J.
Healy, James S.
Hickey, Patrick J.
Hill, Wm. D.
Hitchcock, Harry S.
Hoefler, Benjamin
Jones, John B.
Kaiser, Charles F.
Keane, Wm. H., Meriden.
Kelly, Robert H.
Kelly, Thomas F.
Killoy, Lawrence F.
Keefe, Patrick J.
Kehoe, Thomas J.
Kenney, Thomas
Kenny, John E.
Kinsella, Gerald F.
Kolet, Frank, Meriden.
Kramer, Wm. C., Meriden.
Kuran, Riley B., Torrington.
Langshore, Harry W.
Lawler, Bernard F., Winsted.

Leary, Dennis D., New London.
Lockert, John E., Wallingford.
Lackery, Frederick
Lonergan, Michael
Loventhal, Charles. Promoted to Corporal.
Loy, Clarence W., Meriden.
Lyke, Harvey
Lawrence, Norman F.
Leary, John J.
Leonard, Francis J.
Lynch, Patrick J.
Maher, Cornelius
Maher, Joseph M.
Mahoney, Michael
Marvin, Frank, New Britain.
Masterson, Thomas E. Discharged, disability, July 31st.
McGrath, Richard H.
McNamara, John J. Promoted to Sergeant.
McKinnon, Daniel T.
McLaughlin, Thomas J., Wallingford.
McNeil, Bernard
Meehan, William J., Torrington.
Merli, Edgar A.
Marshall, Robert W.
Merrett, William S.
Miller, Frank W., Torrington.
Mulligan, Lawrence H.
Murphy, Charles F., Naugatuck.
Murray, Thomas A.
Mutz, Hugo
Morton, Edward F.
McMahon, James J.
Mahoney, John S.
O'Connor, Charles A.
O'Donnell, Thomas J.
O'Hare, Raymond. Wallingford.
O'Donnell, Wm. H.

O'Neil, John T.
Parker, Philip E.
Parsons, Matthew F., Torrington.
Phalen, James J.
Rafter, John F.
Reidy, Morris J., Winsted.
Robertson, Wallace C. (Died Oct. 14th.)
Reilly, Patrick H.
Roos, Birger
Ryan, Michael
Richards, Dominick
Richardson, Brodie J., Torrington.
Sabins, Benjamin J.
Sabins, Charles M.
Schomburg, Otto, Wallingford. (Died at home Oct. 2d.)   •
Schultz, Charles E., Winsted.
Scranton, Leonard L.
Scully, Andrew J.
Scully, William J., Torrington.
Seery, James E.
Smiley, Bertram E., Torrington.
Steppler, Charles G.
Stickney, Herbert F.
Stoddard, James C. Promoted to Sergeant.
Sullivan, John F.
Sullivan, James J.
Sweeney, John F.
Toes, Charles H.
Watson, Charles W.
Welch, Merritt
Wesson, John P.
Willey, Joseph A.
Walker, David M. Dishonorably discharged Aug. 22d, order dept. east.
Yorke, Richard B., New London.
Young, Anthony E., Meriden.

MUSTER ROLL

OF THE

Third Regiment Connecticut Volunteer Infantry.

Mustered into the U. S. Service at Niantic, July 2–6, 1898. *Mustered out at Savannah, Ga., March 20, 1899.*

Field and Staff.

Colonel Augustus C. Tyler (resigned; discharged January 31, 1899), ... New London.
Lieutenant-Colonel Alexander Rodgers (promoted to Colonel January 31, 1899), ... Washington, D. C.
Major Henry J. Thayer (resigned; mustered out September 9th), ... Putnam.
Major Gilbert L. Fitch (resigned September 19th), . Stamford.
First Lieutenant and Adjutant Roswell D. Trimble (promoted to Major October 31st), . . New London.
First Lieutenant and Quartermaster Percy H. Morgan, Poquonock.
Major .and Surgeon Julian La Pierre (resigned; mustered out September 21st), ... Norwich.
First Lieutenant and Assistant Surgeon Hiram B. Thomson (promoted to Major and Surgeon September 23d), ... New London.
First Lieutenant and Assistant Surgeon Harry M. Lee, New London.
Assistant Surgeon John S. Blackmar (appointed October 3d), ... Norwich.
Chaplain J. Spencer Voorhees, ... Hartford.

Non-Commissioned Staff.

Sergeant-Major Richard P. Freeman, Jr., New London. Discharged Sept. 8th.
Quartermaster-Sergeant James D. Copp, New London. Discharged September 8th.
Chief Musician Charles H. Phillips, New London. Reduced to ranks.
Principal Musician Aubrey J. Newburg, New London.
Hospital Steward Clarence D. Sevin, Norwich.
Hospital Steward Harry F. Thompson, New London.
Hospital Steward Hubert F. Pierce, East Norwalk.

Company A, of New London.

Captain Henry S. Dorsey.
1st Lieutenant Edward T. Drea. Resigned Nov. 28th.
2d Lieutenant Edward H. Corcoran.
1st Sergeant Frank A. McDonald.
Quartermaster-Sergeant John A. Malona, Waterford.
Sergeant Hubert W. Ryan. Reduced to ranks.
Sergeant John J. Lawless, Waterford. Promoted to 1st Sergeant; promoted to 2d Lieutenant Co. D.
Sergeant Walter W. Philbrick.
Sergeant Edward A. Lawless, Waterford.
Corporal Daniel A. Rankin.

Corporal Sidney E. Morton. Reduced to ranks.

Corporal Edward Pendleton. Reduced to ranks. Promoted to Corporal.

Corporal John T. Sweeney. Reduced to ranks.

Corporal Joseph D. Phillips, Waterford. Reduced to ranks.

Corporal Edward C. Smith. Reduced to ranks.

Corporal Jeremiah T. Moriarty. Reduced to ranks. Promoted to Corporal.

Musician Frank Joseph.

Privates.

Buell, Fred N., Plymouth. Promoted to Corporal.

Breen, Michael E.

Berardinelli, Peter S., Waterford. Discharged January 24th.

Bivens, James M., Tarrytown, Md. Discharged Aug. 24th.

Bunnell, Herbert, Noank.

Bryan, John, Toronto, Can.

Boyle, John, South Windsor.

Barber, Frederick, Chester.

Burr, Clayton W., Chester.

Bennett, Lewis L., Shelton.

Caracausa, Joseph

Chapman, Edward K., Groton.

Carney, Thomas

Carey, Patrick J., Stonington. Promoted to Corporal.

Crowther, Fred, Shelton. Promoted to Corporal.

Coon, Willard E., Westerly, R. I.

Callahan, Charles L., Hartford.

Chapman, Andrew G., Norwich.

Cleveland, Robert I.

Cotter, John F., New Britain.

Drudy, John D. Promoted to Corporal.

Dunn, Daniel F.

Delap, George T.

Deffley, James E.

Dorey, John, Hartford.

Daley, Hugh, Willimantic.

Dykes, James, Shelton.

Doyle, Joseph M.

Foley, Michael

Flynn, John I., Meriden.

Gillespie, Daniel J., Oswego, N. Y.

Greenman, Joseph

Gardineer, George W., Hartford. Promoted to Corporal.

Greer, Benjamin

Hynds, John J.

Higgins, Nicholas D., Rahway, N. J.

Hewie, Ralph, Hartford. Deserted Aug. 13th.

Howard, William, Hartford.

Howard, Joseph.

Hardiman, Thomas C., Bloomfield.

Holland, Arthur, Westerly, R. I.

Holland, James B., Hartford.

Hansen, Gilbert A., Shelton.

Jaeger, Robert H. Promoted to Corporal.

Kay, Benjamin F., Groton. Promoted to Corporal.

Kempf, Frank A., Pomfret. Promoted to Corporal.

Kopp, George

Locke, David M., Boston, Mass.

Lacey, Thomas V., New Britain.

McCarthy, Robert J. Dishonorably discharged.

Mead, Harry A., Portchester, N. Y. Transferred to regimental band Sept. 28th.

Mealady, Daniel J.

Morgan, Charles L., Montville.

McLaughlin, James H. Deserted Sept. 1st.

McPartland, James F., Waterbury.

Martin, Frederick J., Hartford.

Meehan, Michael W., New York, N. Y.

Maloney, William, Derby.

McMoran, Eugene

O'Connell, William, Westerly, R. I.

O'Rourke, Edward J.

O'Rourke, Thomas. Dishonorably discharged.

Oakley, Erastus G., Southport. Promoted to Corporal.

Petty, George

Perrin, Frederick A. Promoted to Corporal.

Powers, Wm. P., Hartford. Dishonorably discharged.

Phair, Michael, Derby.

Reagen, Mert E., Willimantic. Appointed Wagoner.

Rhodes, Wm. H., Wakefield, R. I. Discharged Aug. 24th.

Ryan, John F.

Rogers, Edward H., East Lyme.

Sullivan, Dennis D.

Sullivan, James. Dishonorably discharged.

Sheridan, John J.

Sheridan, Wm. J.

Storey, Wm. J. Deserted Nov. 11th.

Saunders, Lyman R., Mystic.

Skinner, John O.

Shea, Daniel F.

Sauter, John F., Norwich.

Sheehan, Jeremiah, Hartford.

Turk, Harry

Tumelty, Thomas

Tracy, Wm. D. Promoted to Corporal.

Wolverton, Walter H., Noank. Appointed Artificer.

Wilson, John.

Wilson, Wm. Dishonorably discharged.

Williard, Arthur I.. Appointed Musician.

Weinstein, Joseph.

Wright, Fred C., Pomfret. Discharged Feb. 6, 1899.

Watson, Wm. L., Hartford. Dishonorably discharged.

Woods, John E., New Britain.

Waldron, James E., Wallingford. Dishonorably discharged.

Company B, of Pawcatuck.

Captain Cornelius Bransfield, Westerly, R. I.

1st Lieutenant John F. Murphy, Pawcatuck. Promoted to Captain Co. L Nov. 22d.

2d Lieutenant Isaac F. Gavitt.

1st Sergeant James F. Spellman.

Quartermaster Sergeant Esbon H. Gavitt.

Sergeant James J. Murphy. Promoted to 2d Lieutenant Co. H Jan. 22d.

Sergeant John J. Bentley.

Sergeant Patrick W. Shea.

Sergeant Michael F. O'Connell.

Corporal Thomas F. 'Lenihan. Discharged February 13, 1899.

Corporal John T. Fitzgerald.

Corporal John H. Shea.

Corporal Cornelius L. Shea.

Corporal Joseph Herbst, Westerly, R. I.

Corporal James P. McMahon.

Corporal James D. Neville.

Corporal Dennis F. Connell.

Corporal Robert Brucher, Westerly, R. I. Died Nov. 14th.

Corporal Edward W. Murphy, Westerly, R. I.

Corporal John J. Donahue.

Corporal James M. Lindsay.

Musician John J. Cunningham.

Artificer Dennis C. Brown.

Wagoner James J. McCort, Stonington. Reduced to ranks.

Privates.

Angley, Frank J., Abington, Mass.

Alves, Charles, Stonington.

Ahern, Henry P., Norwich.

Bramble, Louis, Shannock, R. I. Deserted.

Barlow, Nathan F., Westerly, R. I.

Brucker, Frank, Westerly, R. I.

Buck, Henry H. Deserted.

Brightman, Frank, Stonington.

Burke, James, Lewiston, Me. Discharged January 16, 1899.

Barry, Joseph, Norwich.

Brown, Juan F., Stafford Springs. Discharged January 29, 1899.

Boles, John, Jr.

Church, Walter, Stafford.

Chadwick, Charles R. Appointed Musician.

Chadwick, James F., Westerly, R. I.

Chadwick, John B., Westerly, R. I.

Chadwick, Wm. F., Westerly, R. I.

Carson, Edward R., Stonington.

Carey, John E.

Carey, Oliver, Stafford Springs.

Casey, Daniel J. Appointed Wagoner.

Casey, John F.

Casey, John

Coleman, Thomas D., Westerly, R. I.

Connell, Patrick H. Promoted to Corporal.

Calmie, Joseph, Westerly, R. I.

Clarke, Edward A., Stafford Springs. Discharged February 6, 1899.

Creighton, James, Blackstone, Mass.

Connor, James J., Norwich.

Connors, John, Providence, R. I.

Donahue, James F.

Donahue, Michael E.

Donahue, John F.

Doran, Andrew E., Manchester.

Duncan, Ernest, Stafford.

Dowling, Thaddeus, Jersey Heights, N. J.

Eaton, Ervin J.

Ennis, John, Stonington.

Farrell, John E.

Fenton, Edwin H.

Fallon, John, Stonington.

Fairfield, David M. Transferred to band.

Fogarty, William L., Norwich. Dishonorably discharged.

Griffin, John, Boston, Mass. Dishonorably discharged.

Gilmore, Dennis, Stonington.

Gould, Ezra, Monson, Mass. Promoted to Corporal.

Hakes, Arlington O., Westerly, R. I.

Harrington, Walter A., Providence, R. I.

Holland, Bert E. Transferred to band.

Jordan, Andrew A., Westerly, R. I. Discharged Feb. 7, 1899.

Kinney, William, Ashaway, R. I.

Knight, Wm. B.

Keegan, John H.

Knowles, George E., No. Stonington.

Lawton, Lewis H., Stafford. Discharged Aug. 8th.

Luck, Gussie A.
Leriche, Wm. H., Westerly, R. I.
Loranger, Omer, Tilton, N. H.
Moriarty, John F., Westerly, R. I. Promoted to Corporal.
Maxson, John W., Stonington. Discharged Nov. 18th, disability.
McDonald, John J.
McDonald, Thomas J.
McGrath, Martin, Westerly, R. I.
McGrath, John D.
McKay, Robert. Transferred to Company I. Promoted to Corporal. Transferred to N. C. S. December 14th as Sergeant-Major.
McQuard, James
O'Gara, James P.
Palmer, Henry E. Discharged Jan. 16, 1899.
Preston, Roger A.
Quiel, Charles, Stafford.
Rabdeau, Joe, Stafford Springs.
Rushlow, Joseph T.
Robinson, Henry, Stonington.
Roche, Patrick D. Promoted to Corporal.
Ryan, John T., Westerly, R. I.
Shea, Daniel C.
Shea, Daniel, Stonington.
Sutton, James, Stonington.
Sullivan, Edward J.
Sullivan, Cornelius, Westerly, R. I.
Smith, Joseph
Tedford, Robert, Stonington.
Whalen, John J.
Wilcox, Jerome A., Stonington. Deserted.
Wright, Robert W., Derby.
White, Thomas F., Lawrence, Mass.
Vitenheimer, Albert H., Derby. Promoted to Sergeant-Major. Promoted to 2d Lieutenant Dec. 8th.

Company C, of Norwich.

Captain Charles A. Hagberg.
1st Lieutenant Harry E. Comstock.
2d Lieutenant Frank Q. Smith.
1st Sergeant Milo R. Waters.
Quartermaster-Sergeant John Gembel.
Sergeant John A. Hagberg. Promoted to 1st Lieutenant, Co. B, Nov. 22d.
Sergeant Charles A. Polsten. Reduced to ranks.
Sergeant Edward T. Waterman.
Sergeant Charles E. Ramage, Montville. Discharged Feb. 2, 1899.
Corporal Charles H. Thorpe, Uncasville. Promoted to Sergeant.
Corporal Wm. C. Zelze. Discharged Feb. 2, 1899.

Corporal Alfred A. S. L'Heureux, Taftville. Reduced to ranks.
Corporal James N. Clark, Jr. Reduced to ranks.
Corporal John Hubbard. Discharged Oct. 10th.
Corporal Frederick W. Burton.
Corporal George W. Rathbun. Discharged Feb. 2, 1899.
Corporal Henry H. Morrill. Promoted to Sergeant.
Corporal Charles Sabrowski.
Musician Leopold A. Grzywacz. Transferred to band.

Privates.

Audette, Elmer, Taftville.
Audette, Alfred, Taftville.
Aspinall, Henry
Ahern, Wm. H.
Bauman, John
Benjamin, James H.
Bliven, George L., Lebanon. Discharged Sept. 6th.
Barnes, Philo H., Preston.
Brock, Eugene S.
Chase, Walter M. Transferred to Co. D; appointed Musician.
Coffee, Walter C. Promoted to Corporal. Promoted to Sergeant.
Casey, Daniel C.
Coles, George D. B., Springfield, Mass.
Corcoran, Murty, Taftville.
Cox, Thomas J.
Caruthers, Wm.
Connell, Patrick F.
Cahoon, David A.
Carter, John
Callahan, Dennis
Callahan, John F. Discharged Feb. 3, 1899.
Carroll, Wm. F., Preston.
Comstock, James H. Transferred to band.
Dyrdal, Giordi
Duff, Daniel. Promoted to Corporal.
Durley, Frank, Greeneville.
Donahue, Patrick H. Appointed Artificer.
Fletcher, Wm. C. Discharged Jan. 24, 1899.
Fletcher, George H. Promoted to Corporal.
Foren, John M., Jewett City.
Fitzgerald, Frederick
Gambel, John, Taftville. Died Sept. 19th.
Gay, James M.
Gadle, George H. Appointed Wagoner.

Gibson, Herbert A. Promoted to Corporal.
Grover, Anson E., Preston.
Geary, Morris F., Montville.
Haselden, John W. Promoted to Corporal.
Hughes, Joseph
Hiscox, Judson L., Preston.
Jack, James, Jr., Greeneville. Promoted to Corporal.
Jeffers, Walter B. S., Jewett City. Promoted to Corporal.
Kellogg, Walter J.
King, Joseph W.
L'Heureux, Nelson S., Taftville.
Loffler, John T.
Lynch, George H., Preston. Discharged Nov. 27, 1898.
Lumsden, George R.
Letendre, George, Taftville.
Maguire, Wm. F.
Malone, Wm. J., Taftville.
McClure, Wm., Preston.
McVey, Peter
Merrill, Orville W., Springfield, Mass.
Miner, Huburt, Greeneville.
Moore, Michael M. Promoted to Corporal. Reduced to ranks.
Morgan, James, Jr.
McGill, John H., Stamford. Discharged Jan. 3, 1899.
McCormick, James, Maysville, Ky.
Mausmann, Andrew H., Franklin.
Olsson, Ivar, Greeneville.
Osborne, John C. Appointed Musician.
Oliver, Charles B.
Perkins, Charles T. Promoted to Corporal.
Peckham, Wm. W. Transferred to band.
Pierce, Arthur W., Jewett City.
Pigott, John J., Northfield. Promoted to Corporal.
Pickorski, Mike
Reeves, George P., Taftville.
Robinson, Walter C. Appointed Musician.
Rushlow, Peter
Rathbun, Charles I. Transferred to band.
Raphael, Robert, Montville.
Sabrowski, August. Discharged Jan. 24, 1899.
Sellick, Frederick W.
Sikorski, Albert
Sikorski, John, Greeneville.
Simpson, Louis E., Franklin.
Skinner, Benjamin F.
Sterry, Frank E. Promoted to Corporal.

Stark, Wm., Brattleboro, Vt. Discharged Jan. 30, 1899.
Sullivan, Patrick, Taftville.
Taft, Frank G., Glen Falls, N. Y.
Thorp, Albert. Promoted to Corporal.
Thorpe, Wm. H., Montville. Promoted to Corporal.
Tooker, Frederick B. Transferred to band.
Turner, George A.
Tylendar, Antoni
Woodworth, Harvey L.
Welden, Albert C.

Company D, of New London.

Captain David Conner, New London.
1st Lieutenant Wm. H. Ryley, New London. Discharged Jan. 24, 1899.
2d Lieutenant Charles P. Kirkland. Promoted to Captain Co. M, Sept. 11th.
1st Sergeant George Hennes.
Quartermaster-Sergeant Emmett L. Crowell.
Sergeant Frank L. Beckwith. Reduced to ranks.
Sergeant Carlos G. Champlin. Transferred to Co. H, 2d U. S. Vols. Engineers, Dec. 6th.
Sergeant Wm. R. Chipman. Promoted to 1st Sergeant.
Corporal Joseph J. Carr. Reduced to ranks. Dishonorably discharged Feb. 18, 1899.
Corporal Daniel B. Scoville. Reduced to ranks.
Corporal Harry B. Prince. Reduced to ranks.
Corporal John J. Butler.
Corporal Frank J. Martin.
Corporal Michael F. Hogan, North Plains. Deserted Oct. 13th.
Corporal Michael C. Carey.
Corporal John F. Conway.
Corporal Byron W. Bemis, Shelton. Promoted to Sergeant.
Musician George E. Ryley. Reduced to ranks; promoted to Corporal.
Musician Charles Ormsby.
Wagoner Cassius A. Harding.

Privates.

Albecker, Edward, Brooklyn, N. Y.
Allen, Henry, Norwich.
Austin, James, Shelton. Deserted July 20th.
Asselin, Joseph E. W., Webster, Mass. Transferred to Signal Corps, U. S. V.

Burdick, Edwin S., Escoheag, R. I.
Buck, Leon F., Stamford. Promoted to Corporal.
Buchannan, John, Pomfret.
Blackledge, John T., Brooklyn, N. Y.
Condoff, William, New Haven.
Cunningham, Robert W., New Haven.
Corr, Daniel, Waterbury. Deserted Dec. 16.
Culloo, Wm. F., Stamford.
Conroy, James H., Stamford.
Conklin, Lincoln, Stamford. Promoted to Corporal.
Cullen, Henry B., Ansonia. Promoted to Sergeant.
Creighton, Thomas J., Woonsocket, R. I.
Dean, George, Bridgeport.
Daley, Edward, Haverhill, Mass. Deserted Oct. 28th.
Dutton, Joel A.
Dayton, Frank E., Bridgeport.
Devaney, Stephen H., Bridgeport. Dishonorably discharged.
Fleming, Wm. J., Pittsfield. Mass.
Fitzpatrick, Daniel, Stamford.
Gould, Everett
Guile, Otis S.
Garde, James, New Haven. Deserted Nov. 11th.
Gifford, Edward L., Derby. Discharged Dec. 29th.
Gorman, Edward C., Bridgeport. Discharged Aug. 18th.
Galligan, Michael J., New Haven. Promoted to Corporal. Reduced to ranks.
Holloway, Daniel W., New Haven. Promoted to Corporal; deserted Sept. 26th.
Hagan, John J., Stamford. Promoted to Corporal.
Hearns, John R., Stamford.
Hedman, Charles J., Stamford.
Higgins, Richard, Bridgeport. Deserted.
Hickey, James. Transferred to U. S. V. Signal Corps Feb. 18, 1899.
Keeney, Patrick, Philadelphia, Pa.
King, Edward J., Stamford. Dishonorably discharged March 7th.
Kane, John J., Derby. Discharged Nov. 27th.
Lynch, Thomas F., Waterbury.
Lee, James T., Norwich. Discharged Aug. 18th.
Monohan, John E., New Haven.
Millard, Leonard D., New Haven.
Miner, Charles A. Deserted Dec. 7.
Maher, Thomas F., New Haven. Promoted to Corporal.
Martin, Edward, Stamford.
Moore, Wm. P., Stamford.

Mitchell, George D. New York. Deserted Sept. 15th.
McFarland, John H., Montville.
Morgan, Harry E.
McMahon, Thomas H., Holyoke, Mass. Promoted to Corporal.
McCann, Joseph, Bridgeport.
Neff, Frank P., Waterford.
O'Brien, James, New Britain.
O'Neil, John E., New Haven.
O'Keefe, James F., Greenwich. Promoted to Corporal.
O'Connor, Michael, Stamford.
Preston, Wm. F., New Haven.
Polskey, Joseph, Montville.
Pellett, Lewis E., Scotland.
Pry, Joshua J., Montville. Discharged Aug. 24th.
Russell, John, North Grosvenordale.
Roberts, Samuel E., Stamford.
Reynolds, James B., Stamford.
Roberts, David, Stamford. Promoted to Corporal.
Rafferty, Joseph F., Stamford.
Rinaldi, James, Stamford.
Rudd, John S.
Rutter, Edward V., Lancaster, O.
Rooney, John, Bridgeport.
Stebbins, Charles S., East Lyme.
Stinchfield, Walter P.
Stillenworth, Everett. Promoted to Corporal.
Sydney, Arthur J., Greenwich.
Sullivan, Peter, Stamford.
Sullivan, Dennis J., Durham. Appointed Artificer.
Sullivan, Philip A., New Haven.
Spooner, Isaac F., Springfield, Mass.
Sherry, Thomas, Waterford.
Slater, Charles E., Shelton. Promoted to Corporal.
Thewlis, Thomas J., Stamford.
Thompson, Linneus M. Transferred to U. S. V., Signal, Corps, Jan. 14, 1899.
Tobin, John E., Stamford.
Terleski, John, Webster, Mass.
Voos, Charles, East Bridgeport.
Warner, Carl, Springfield. Deserted Aug. 15th.
Wilson, Arthur G., Stamford.
White, Martin, Stamford.
Willey, Frank, Norwich.
Wright, George H. Promoted to Corporal; promoted to Sergeant.

Company E, of Willimantic.

Captain Edward F. Flynn. Resigned October 1st.
1st Lieutenant James Cochrane. Promoted to Captain October 15th.

29

2d Lieutenant Michael Cronin. Re-
signed Oct. 7th.
1st Sergeant William Kelley.
Quartermaster-Sergeant Michael J.
Murphy.
Sergeant Timothy Kelley. Reduced to
ranks.
Sergeant James J. Sullivan.
Sergeant Maurice J. Sullivan. Reduced
to ranks.
Sergeant Andrew Faulds.
Corporal James English. Reduced to
ranks.
Corporal Edward F. Corrigan. Dis-
charged Dec. 20th.
Corporal Michael D. Sullivan. Re-
duced to ranks. Promoted to Cor-
poral.
Corporal John Simmons.
Corporal John J. Kelly.
Corporal Michael J. English.
Corporal William Falvey.
Corporal Frank P. Fenton.
Corporal James F. Lynch. Reduced to
ranks.
Corporal Timothy McNamara. Pro-
moted to Sergeant.
Corporal Jean B. Paullins.
Corporal James H. Walsh.
Musician Michael J. Sullivan. Ap-
pointed Wagoner.
Musician George Haggerty.

Privates.

Ashton, Louis. Promoted to Corporal.
Benway, Peter H.
Bland, Charles E.
Bliven, John L., Eagleville.
Brown, John, Jr., Mansfield.
Bump, Fred T. Promoted to Corporal.
Caillonette, Octave. Promoted to Ser-
geant; transferred to band.
Caillonette, Eli. Deserted Oct. 10th.
Cairns, John
Casey, James
Casey, Wm. S.
Clancy, Michael
Curran, Patrick
Daley, James J.
Darby, Fred. Discharged Sept. 8th.
Davis, Fred. (Died Oct. 27th.)
Demarais, Joseph
Donahue, Joseph F.
Donahue, Patrick
Edgarton, John B. Discharged Jan. 23,
1899.
Fenton, Anson C.
Fenton, James
Fraser, Paul S.
Gillette, Samuel
Gingras, John B.

Guilford, Joseph E.
Goff, Willis H.
Hagan, James F.
Hoey, John
Hoffman, Alvin C.
Hussey, Daniel
Hyde, Albert B.
Johnstone, William. Appointed Arti-
ficer.
Joyce, Thomas
King, William
Lacey, George P., South Coventry.
Lacroix, John. (Died Oct. 10th.)
Larrabee, Christopher A., Windham.
Lavezzi, David
Laflamme, Joseph
Loomis, Herbert L. Discharged Feb.
10, 1899.
Lynch, Edward J. Promoted to Cor-
poral.
Marra, Thomas E.
Maxwell, Wm. J. Discharged Feb. 20,
1899.
Maynard, Joseph
McCarthy, John T. Promoted to Cor-
poral.
McCarthy, Jeremiah A.
McCabe, Patrick, Derby.
McGee, Patrick, Ansonia.
Morean, Frederick H.
Moriarty, Thomas F.
Meigs, Clifton O., Niantic.
Murphy, Edward A. Deserted Dec. 2d.
Mullen, Samuel
Morse, Ernest, Shelton.
Moran, James
Norton, Wm. J.
O'Brien, John F., South Coventry.
O'Keefe, Edward J.
Owens, Thomas
Pates, James W. R. Deserted Nov. 6th.
Perry, Isaac P.
Quinn, Timothy
Reede, Patrick, Derby.
Regan, Bernard
Shea, James J.
Smith, Alexander
Smith, Willard. Deserted Dec. 22d.
Sullivan, Jeremiah P. Discharged Jan.
24, 1899.
Sullivan, Jerry J.
Sullivan, Michael J.
Sullivan, James
Sullivan, John F.
Sullivan, James D. Promoted to Cor-
poral.
Sullivan, Lawrence D.
Sweet, Arthur W.
Sweet, Frederick A.
Tully, William H. Promoted to Cor-
poral.

Tarrent, Joseph
Teevan, Frank
Whitehouse, Frank
Wilcox, Edward L.
Wilcox, Wells S., South Coventry.
Windmiller, Everett
Wood, Fred
Ward, Frederick H. Appointed Artificer; died Nov. 6th.

Company F, of Danielson.

Captain Wm. H. Hamilton.
1st Lieutenant Kent A. Darbie.
2d Lieutenant Clarence E. Young. Promoted to 1st Lieutenant, Co. H, Oct. 15th; discharged Feb. 10, 1899.
1st Sergeant Frederick N. Flagg.
Quartermaster-Sergeant Eddy U. G. Baker.
Sergeant Wm. A. Hoyle. Promoted to Quartermaster-Sergeant.
Sergeant Wm. H. Warren.
Sergeant Frank E. Young.
Sergeant Philip Lockwood.
Corporal Carl Anderson.
Corporal Louis F. Roberts, Wauregan.
Corporal Herbert H. Flagg.
Corporal Andrew C. Racine, Dayville. Promoted to Sergeant.
Corporal Alfred C. Cutler.
Corporal Fred Nash.
Corporal John L. Kingsbury, Ballouville. Reduced to ranks.
Corporal James E. Harrington.
Corporal Joseph A. Lapelle. Reduced to ranks.
Corporal George H. Farron.
Corporal Samuel N. Frink, Moosup.
Corporal Fred Bowen, Sterling.
Musician Clarence W. Bacon. Transferred to band.
Musician John Levell. Transferred to band.
Wagoner Edwin Saunders, East Killingly. Discharged Jan. 26th.

Privates.

Asselin, Oscar L., Sterling.
Bailey, Gilbert A. (Died Oct. 13th.)
Bates, Arthur E., Monson, Mass.
Benoit, Napoleon
Boirin, Adolph, Wauregan.
Brooks, Clarence C., Dedham. Mass.
Browne, Charles V., South Killingly.
Burke, George, Wauregan.
Chartrand, Dona, Shelton. Deserted Dec. 22d.
Clark, John M., Ansonia.
Colleran, John P., Fall River, Mass.

Condon, James, Jr., New Haven.
Coogan, Patrick, Jewett City. Dishonorably discharged
Copeland, Harry B., Brooklyn.
Copeland, James C., Brooklyn.
Curran, John J., Dayville.
Daignault, Fred I., Wauregan.
Dillon, John E., Lafayette, R. I. Promoted to Corporal.
Duke, Frank W. F.
Dwyer, Martin J., Wauregan. Dishonorably discharged.
Earnshaw, Albert B., Dayville. Discharged Dec. 14th.
Fagnant, Hector G., Hope, R. I. Deserted Oct. 13th.
Ferneal, Fred
Fogal, Charles, Southbridge, Mass. Dishonorably discharged.
Fournier, Domas
Gaffney, Thomas. Appointed Musician.
Gagnon, Frank, Auburn, Me.
Ganthier, Delor, Wauregan. Appointed Artificer.
Gay, Everett E., Attawaugan. Discharged Jan. 24th.
Germain, Philip, Dayville.
Gibson, Frank I., North Sterling. Promoted to Corporal.
Gilman, John H., Attawaugan.
Golden, William, Saint Francis, Me.
Greene, Hosea. Appointed Musician.
Gregoire, Medas, Wauregan.
Hamilton, Cassius A. Appointed Wagoner.
Head, Michael J., Jr.
Hines, Charles D., North Sterling.
Hughes, Daniel P., Attawaugan.
Hurley, Stephen, Willimantic. Deserted Dec. 30th.
Howard, Charles B.
Irons, Lewis, Moosup.
Johnson, Francis H., Plainfield.
Jolly, James K., Norwich.
Jordan, George W., Warwick, R. I. Deserted Dec. 22d.
Kennedy, Charles A.
Laramie, Bartimus J., Attawaugan.
Lavell, James, Fall River, Mass.
Larence, George A., Putnam.
Lofgren, John, Wauregan. Promoted to Corporal.
Lyman, Ernest C.
Malbone, James H., Brooklyn. Promoted to Corporal.
Marley, James, Webster, Mass.
Matthews, Elmer J., Westford.
Monahan, James, Moosup. Discharged Jan. 24, 1899.
Monahan, Patrick, Moosup. Discharged Jan. 28, 1899.

Maynard, George, Wauregan.
McDonald, George, Wauregan.
McDermott, Thomas J.
McGirney, Patrick, Ansonia.
McKay, Robert B., Seymour.
McRan, William, Wauregan. Dishonorably discharged.
Moran, George, Ansonia.
Mottram, John T., New Bedford, Mass. Deserted Aug. 6th.
Morse, Albert H., Wauregan.
McShane, Michael, East Killingly.
Oban, Felix, Wauregan.
Perkins, George H., South Killingly. Deserted Aug. 31st.
Popple, George A.
Potter, Ezekiel I.., Killingly.
Quinn, Michael A. Discharged Jan. 27th.
Rapp, Charles C.
Rooney, Michael F. Deserted Oct. 13th.
Roberts, Napoleon F., Wauregan.
Rosebush, Hersey J.
Schlitter, Ernest W., Ansonia.
Sholes, Herbert E., Ballouville.
Sullivan, Frank, Williamsville.
Tracy, Gurdon F., Wauregan.
Walker, Frederick E., Willimantic.
Warren, Frank J.
Watt, Robert, Cohoes, N. Y.
Webster, Lester A. Discharged Feb. 3d.
Wood, John, Moosup.
Young. Fred, Williamsville. Deserted.

Company G, of Putnam.

Captain Arthur D. McIntyre.
1st Lieutenant Charles E. Richardson.
2d Lieutenant Everett M. Carver. Promoted to 1st Lieutenant, Co. A, Dec. 9th.
1st Sergeant George W. Wilbur.
Quartermaster-Sergeant Wm. F. Holt. Promoted to Quartermaster-Sergeant N. C. S.
Sergeant Frank L. Main. Promoted to Quartermaster-Sergeant.
Sergeant Stephen Brady.
Sergeant Clarence W. Chase.
Corporal Joseph Breault. Promoted to Sergeant.
Corporal Adin A. Harrington. Promoted to Sergeant.
Corporal George G. Milliken.
Corporal William A. Hall. Reduced to ranks.
Corporal George Lamondy.
Corporal Charles St. Onge.
Corporal Walter R. Quinn. Reduced to ranks.

Corporal Fred E. Kies. Reduced to ranks.
Corporal Grant S. Hopkins.
Corporal Thomas W. Duffy.
Corporal Felix King.
Corporal Leroy E. Tourtellotte.
Musician Ralph P. Durfee. Promoted to Quartermaster-Sergeant; transferred to band as Principal Musician.
Musician John B. Mayo.
Artificer Carl Aug. Larson, N. Grosvenordale.
Wagoner Stanley S. Watson, Pomfret. Reduced to ranks.

Privates.

Bailey, Elmer C.
Blake, Wm. H.
Benway, Peter
Blanchette, Herman
Brouillette, Pierre C.
Burrows, Horace W. Discharged Jan. 9, 1899.
Brett, James
Bibeau, David, Arctic Center, R. I.
Bellrose, Ulric
Barnes, C. Harry, Pottsdam, N. Y.
Beaudry, Harry N., Grosvenordale.
Broadhurst, George E. Appointed Musician. -
Brady, Ambrose J.
Benoit, Juter. Discharged Jan. 19, 1899, disability.
Beaudry, Joseph, Grosvenordale.
Cautwell, James. Norwich.
Connors, Wm., Webster, Mass.
Corbin, Charles S., Webster, Mass. Discharged without honor, Feb. 8, 1899.
Cardinal, Louis, Killingly.
Cruise, Frank J., Pascoag, R. I. Promoted to Corporal.
Cunningham, Patrick, Ashuelot, N. H.
Cutter. Phineas, Nashua, N. H. Promoted to Corporal.
Cutler, Augustus
Converse, Henry L.
Champeau, Albert
Dion, Israel P., Webster, Mass.
Duffey, James H.
Debosher, Joseph
Devlin, Wm. J., Gilbertville, Mass.
Downs, William S.
Droney, Patrick, Providence. R. I.
Dumonchelle, Louis J., Webster, Mass.
Flye, Fred S.
Fall, Willie
Girade, Arthur, North Grosvenordale.
Girade, Napoleon, No. Grosvenordale. (Died Aug. 29th.)

Grinnell, George W.
Garner, Joseph
Gagne, Albert
Gaudette, Arthur
Hahn, George C. (Died Nov. 9th.)
Kent, George M. Promoted to Corporal.
Kozak, Anthony
Loiselle, Alphonse
Lamondy, Thomas
LeClaire, Alfred, Killingly.
Lovely, George
Lowe, Charles W., So. Woodstock. Discharged Jan. 24, 1899.
McCoy, Wm. H.
Madison, Charles W., So. Woodstock
Maloney, Eugene R.
Murphy, Bernard P.
McGann, James E.
Micotte, Charles
Menard, Willie
Moore, Willis E., Woodstock. Appointed Wagoner.
Marion, Joseph
Murray, William J.
Main, Walter, Ashford.
Messier, Louis. Discharged March 9. 1899.
O'Neil, James
Ouillette, Augueste, Moosup.
Plouffe, Doseithee, Webster, Mass. Transferred to band.
Petsching, Charles W., Lymanville, R. I.
Roberts, Charles
Ryan, Edward J.
Reynolds, Bartholomew, Pomfret. Promoted to Corporal.
Rylander, John E., Pomfret. (Died Oct. 7th.)
Richards, Albert, Grosvenordale.
Sharpe, Harry W. Transferred to band; discharged Jan. 16, 1899.
Sherman, Henry A.
St. Martin, Joseph
St. Martin, Stephen
Smith, Charles E., So. Milford, Mass.
St. Onge, Peter
Staples, Lewis, Woodstock.
Sutton, Robert, Uxbridge.
Sweeney, Marshall
Scott, Caleb M., Hampton.
Swett, Hubert N., Pomfret.
Toolan, John J. Promoted to Corporal.
Terry, Robert C.
Travis, Lindley M. Promoted to Corporal.
Tremblay, Henry
Young, George D., So. Woodstock.

Company H,

Recruited at Stonington.

Captain Hadlai A. Hull, Stonington. Promoted to Major Sept. 23d; resigned Oct. 17th.
1st Lieutenant Herbert D. Utley, New London. Resigned Oct. 11th.
2d Lieutenant Walter T. Fish, Mystic. Resigned Jan. 1st; mustered out Jan. 6th.
1st Sergeant Willis N. Hawley, Hawleyville. Died Nov. 19, 1898.
Quartermaster-Sergeant Charles S. Francis, Newington.
Sergeant Herbert Kirkpatrick, Cromwell. Discharged Jan. 24, 1899.
Sergeant Charles S. Chapman, Westbrook.
Corporal Oscar W. Palmer, Norwich. Promoted to 1st Sergeant.
Corporal George M. Greene, Canterbury. Promoted to Sergeant.
Corporal Myron A. Maynard, Jewett City.
Corporal Wilfred Prevost, Jewett City.
Corporal Francis L. Driscoll, Waterbury. Discharged Oct. 12th.
Corporal Albert Simmons, New Haven.
Corporal Philip Isaacs, New Haven. Reduced to ranks.
Corporal John J. Gilmartin, New Haven.
Corporal George E. Hubbard, New Haven. Reduced to ranks.
Musician Charles A. Perkins, Preston. Reduced to ranks.
Wagoner George Conrad, Norwich.

Privates.

Anthony, Gould R. Promoted to Corporal.
Abby, George, North Stonington. Deserted Nov. 19th.
Aldrich, Harry, State Line.
Bassett, Edwin B., Norwich.
Brennan, Humphrey, Norwich.
Barrett, Michael, Hartford.
Beard, Fred B., Willimantic.
Breslin, James, New Haven.
Brotherton, George, New Haven. Promoted to Corporal.
Carroll, John T., Norwich.
Cavanaugh, Patrick, Stonington.
Conrad, John, Preston.
Coughlin, David, Norwich.
Cox, Thomas.
Carrigg, Thomas, New London.
Callahan, Christopher, New London.

Carter, John F., Norwich. Discharged Aug. 22d.
Connors, Patrick T., New Haven.
Curran, James F., New Haven.
Comerford, Michael, Waterbury.
Coleman, Thomas, New Haven.
Cairns, James, New Haven.
Daniels, Richard, Stonington.
Devine, Michael, Jr., Norwich.
Dupois, Joseph O. O. Occum. Deserted Oct. 25th.
Donahue, Michael, New Haven.
Davis, John T., New Haven. Deserted Aug. 16th.
Duane, John W., Danbury.
Dutram, Peter, Bridgeport. Deserted Aug. 14th.
Donnelly, Francis, New Haven.
Dillon, John, Waterbury.
Enright, James F., New Haven.
Flynn, James F., New Haven.
Frid, Charles, Bridgeport.
Foote, Herbert M., New Haven.
Galbraith, Arthur, Norwich. Appointed Artificer.
Gay, Frederick A., Norwich.
Gay, William T., Norwich. Deserted Jan. 28, 1899.
Glass, Harry H., New Haven. Promoted to Corporal.
Gore, Thomas J., New Haven. Deserted.
Greenwood, James F., New Britain.
Hoye, Frank, Danbury.
Heady, Harry, Danbury.
Harrison, Thomas P., Danbury.
Hallesey, Wm., Norwich.
Hayes, Thomas M., New Haven.
Hewlitt, Charles, Lebanon.
Harkins, James, Leominster, Mass.
Healy, Daniel, New London.
Jones, George, New Haven.
Kehr, Wm., Norwich.
Kelly, John N., Norwich.
Keane, Frank, New Haven. Discharged Aug. 22d.
King, Thomas, New Haven.
Kennedy, Richard, Stafford Springs.
Lamb, Walter H., Norwich. Promoted to Corporal.
Lukoski, Joseph, Norwich.
Lyons, Edward, New Haven.
Lee, Wm., New Haven.
Mell, Charles B., Norwich.
Mullaney, John H., Groton.
Murphy, Thomas L., Providence, R. I.
McShera, John P., New Haven.
Moore, Luke
Morris, John S., Danbury. Deserted Nov. 2d.
Moran, Thomas J., Danbury.

Meyers, Julius C., New Haven.
McMahon, Thomas L., New Haven.
O'Neil, Francis, Jr., New Haven.
O'Rouark, John J., Albany, N. Y. Deserted Aug. 13th.
Pariseau, Nelson, Glasgo. Deserted Oct. 25th.
Powers, Ralph F., Norwich. Discharged Aug. 22d.
Rourke, John, Preston.
Reno, Henry, Pinconning, Mich.
Sauter, John, Danbury. Deserted Sept. 21st.
Sullivan, Patrick, Norwich.
Sullivan, John, Fair Haven.
Shannon, Jeremiah, Jewett City.
Sparks, Ernest, Norwich.
Sheehan, Daniel, Jewett City.
Singer, Wm., Danielson. Deserted.
Shea, Patrick J., New Haven.
Slattery, James E., Milford, Mass. Appointed Musician.
Smidt, Emil, Bridgeport. Deserted Jan. 11, 1899.
Smith, George, New Haven. Deserted.
Tregaskis, Hubert A., New Haven. Promoted to Corporal.
Tierney, James W., New Haven.
Wallace, Wm. E., Griswold.
Whipple, Frederick E., Jewett City. Appointed Musician.
Winans, Frank J., Norwich. Promoted to Corporal.
Wood, Eugene, Danbury.

¡Company I, of New London.

Captain Eugene T. Kirkland. Promoted to Major Sept. 11th; Lieutenant-Colonel, Feb. 27, 1899.
1st Lieutenant Albert P. Ware. Promoted to Captain Sept. 11th.
2d Lieutenant Carey Congdon. Promoted to 1st Lieutenant Sept. 15th. Resigned and mustered out Dec. 4th.
2d Lieutenant Daniel Tyler Moore. Appointed Sept. 19th.
1st Sergeant Harris Pendleton, Jr. Promoted to 2d Lieutenant Co. M, July 23d. Promoted to 1st Lieutenant Co. E, Oct. 15th.
Quartermaster-Sergeant John T. Sherwin.
Sergeant Richard B. Smith. Promoted to 1st Sergeant.·
Sergeant Louis H. Goddard.
Corporal Thomas H. Jennings. Promoted to Sergeant. Promoted to 2d Lieutenant Co. M, Nov. 12th.
Corporal Clark S. Bishop. Promoted to Sergeant.

Corporal Jeremiah J. Murphy. Promoted to Sergeant.

Corporal John H. Broadwell.

Corporal John I. Stubbert. Promoted to Sergeant.

Corporal John E. Angus, Groton.

Musician Harry A. Wiley. Discharged Jan. 6th.

Musician Wm. M. Dunn.

Privates.

Allen, William H.

Allen, Lucian O., Mystic.

Baker, Alexander, Woonsocket, R. I. Promoted to Corporal.

Baxter, John, Perryville, Mass. Dishonorably discharged.

Bennett, Patrick. Deserted Aug. 15th.

Berthel, Rudolph C., New Haven.

Berry, Lewis O., Montville.

Bollard, George, Ansonia. Appointed Wagoner.

Blake, Frederick C.

Bruedly, George, Philadelphia, Pa.

Blanchard, Frederick C., Norwich.

Blake, Wm. F., New Haven.

Breen, James, New Haven.

Brobeck, Albert

Butterly, Peter

Callahan, Wm. F. Promoted to Corporal.

Conners, Thomas, Attleboro, Mass. Dishonorably discharged.

Crump, Richard L. Promoted to Corporal; discharged Dec. 17th.

Carroll, Wm., New Haven.

Condon, John J., New Haven. (Died Oct. 14th.)

Conway, Wm. F., New Haven.

Condon, Jeremiah, New Haven.

Coombs, Ralph A., Lincolnville, Me.

Daniels, George I., Saybrook.

Degnan, Joseph M., New Hevan.

Doyle, James F., New Haven.

Dart, Bertie, South Lyme.

Emerson, Thomas R., New Haven.

Fitzpatrick, Joseph, New Haven. .

Farrell, Frank T., Norwich.

Gallagher, James W., New Haven.

Gernhard, Adam J., Norwich. Promoted to Corporal.

Greene, Arthur A., Westerly, R. I. Discharged without honor Dec. 1st.

Gingrass, Frank J., Taftville.

Glennon, John T., New Haven.

Gleason, Wm. J., Norwich.

Gettings, Bernard A., Watertown, N. Y.

Galpin, Charles H., Shelton.   .

Hallock, Willard H., Chester.

Hayes, Stephen J. Promoted to Corporal.

Holmes, Jesse N., Saybrook. (Died Oct. 27th.)

Holmes, Wm. I., Deep River.

Hunter, John A., Jr., Norwichtown.

Hanrahan, John, Norwich.

Heglan, Edward S., New Haven.

Hartigan, Daniel G., New Haven.

James, Frederick H.

Keefe, Denis, Hartford.

Kelleher, Joseph P., New Haven. Dishonorably discharged.

Kelly, James F.

Lock, George, New Haven.

Latham, Albert, Groton.

La Rose, Thomas F., Brooklyn, N. Y.

Murley, Thomas J., Jr., New Haven.

McKegg, Alfred R., New Haven.

Mack, Edward H. Promoted to Corporal.

Malona, Charles. Appointed Artificer.

McGregor, James, Jr., Mystic. Promoted to Corporal.

Mills, John, Waterford. Transferred to Co. C; transferred to Co. D.

Mecklenburg, John J., Ansonia.

Mooney, Wm. P., New Haven.

Murphy, John J., New Haven.

McAvoy, James, New Haven.

Mahoney, Michael J., New Haven.

Myers, Lee, New York city.

Mulligan, Frank

Manning, Thomas J., Shelton. Transferred to N. C. S. Sept. 8th; transferred to Co. L, Nov. 14th.

McCarron, John

Newberg, Harry N., Groton.

Noland, Wm. H. Promoted to Corporal.

O'Brien, Michael P., New Britain.

O'Mara, John, Deep River.

O'Niel, Owen, Norwich.

Parsons, Waldo H.

Parkinson, Joseph, Exeter, N. H. Deserted Oct. 23d.

Pendleton, Lyman B.

Peppin, Frederick, Taftville.

Phillips, Wm. C., New Haven.

Reed, Lorenzo R. Discharged Sept. 2d, disability.

Reed, Winder E., Waterford.

Rockwell, Walter S.

Rehley, Charles, Norwich.

Russell, John C., Jr., New Haven. Promoted to Corporal.

Seaman, Carl

Simmones, Joseph, New Haven. Deserted Oct. 13th.

Smith, Jesse, Groton. Promoted to Corporal.

Slattery, Edward P., New Haven.
Tracy, George, New Haven.
Walsh, William, New Britain. Appointed Musician.
Williams, Frank E., Groton.
Williams, Thomas S.
Willows, Henry L. Promoted to Corporal.
Wolfe, David, Mystic.
Wood, Edmond
Wattles, Wm. M., Shelton.

Company K, of Stamford.

(Co. C, 4th Regiment, C. N. G.)

Captain Philip W. Prior. Promoted to Major.
1st Lieutenant Charles W. Bucklee. Promoted to Captain.
2d Lieutenant Frederick G. C. Smith, Greenwich. Resigned; mustered out Sept. 3d.
1st Sergeant Elmer Weston. Promoted to 2d Lieutenant Sept. 9th; promoted to 1st Lieutenant.
Quartermaster-Sergeant Edwin F. Rambo. Returned to duty from sickness as Sergeant.
Sergeant James W. Smith.
Sergeant Andrew J. Moran, Glenbrook. Promoted to First Sergeant.
Sergeant Wells Weston. Discharged Jan. 3, 1899, disability.
Sergeant Benjamin Stewart.
Corporal Frank B. Gurley, Glenbrook.
Corporal Ira S. Palmer.
Corporal Oliver J. Stewart. Discharged Dec. 23d.
Corporal John A. Maher.
Corporal Peter Murray. Discharged Dec. 10th.
Corporal Frank J. Scully.
Corporal Charles C. Weideman.
Musician Harvey D. Hatch. Promoted to 1st Sergeant; promoted to 2d Lieutenant.

Privates.

Albert, John H., Springdale.
Armstrong, Joseph P.
Baynes, Ernest H. Discharged Oct. 27th.
Bonnell, Joseph F. (Died Oct. 6th.)
Boswell, Wm. S., Greenwich. Promoted to Corporal. Discharged Nov. 4th.
Botsford, John, Jr.
Britt, Gilbert A.
Burk, Thomas F.
Burnett, Harry, Greenwich.
Burns, Edgar J.
Burr, George H.
Caterson, George H., Mt. Vernon, N. Y.
Clarke, John J.
Clark, Walter T. Appointed Musician.
Crawford, Henry P., Greenwich.
Crissey, Henry M., Long Ridge.
Cudlipp, George M.
Curran, John J.
Daley, James A.
Devitt, John E.
Dolan, Patrick, Sound Beach.
Dunne, John J.
Dutcher, Wm. C., Brooklyn, N. Y.
Eccles, Robert J.
Enright, Morgan J.
Fairchild, Wm. H.
Finan, Michael J.
Finch, Edward D. Transferred to band.
Finch, Frederick O.
Fitzpatrick, Francis J.
Flynne, David E.
Giles, Wm. A.
Gill, John J.
Gisborne, Frank R., Riverside. Promoted to Corporal.
Gerard, Frank
Gleason, Edward J.
Greene, Frank H.
Gully, Eugene W.
Hitt, Alfred C. Promoted to Corporal; reduced to ranks.
Hynes, John J. Appointed Musician.
Hynes, Thomas
Isbell, Burt
Johnson, James M.
Kenealy, Edward J.
Kenefic, James E. Promoted to Corporal.
Krafft, Frederick A.
Kurth, Arnold
Lahey, Edward J., Jr.
Law, Thomas F.
Lester, Edward O. Promoted to Corporal.
Maguire, John R.
Mahrt, John
Malin, James F.
Manning, James E.
Martin, John
McClellan, Frank W.
McDonald, Arthur A.
Mead, Seaman M., Greenwich.
Miller, Herbert
Mooney, Michael J. Appointed Wagoner.
Moore, Thomas E.
Mory, Louis, Branford.
Murdock, George W. Promoted to Quartermaster-Sergeant.
Murray, Edward H. Promoted to Corporal.

O'Connor, Terence
O'Neill, James J.
Paight, John H.
Peck, Charles H. Promoted to Corporal.
Peters, John J.
Pierce, John T.
Porter, Bert F. Appointed Artificer.
Raymond, Arthur S.
Raymond, Paul A. Promoted to Corporal.
Reese, James J.
Rew, Fred J.
Ritch, James A. Promoted to Corporal.
Sanborn, Irving L. Discharged Jan. 28, 1899.
Scott, Elmer J., Port Chester, N. Y. Promoted to Corporal. (Died Jan. 28th.)
Slaney, Oliver H. Promoted to Corporal.
Smith, George R., Darien.
Smith, Ralph J., Philadelphia, Pa.
Smith, Robert. Transferred to ·band.
Sparks, John H.
Stankard, John J.
Talbot, Frederick, Greenwich.
Thompson, George R.
Tichenor, Herbert G.
Toms, Leslie R. Transferred to band.
Veit, Frank F.
Weed, Howard F.
Weed, Robert L.
Worden, Harry B.

Company L, of Norwalk.

(Co. F, 4th Regiment, C. N. G.)

Captain Reuben M. Rose. Resigned Oct. 22d.
1st Lieutenant Wm. W. Bloom.
2d Lieutenant Wm. I. Comstock.
1st Sergeant John H. Smith. Reduced to ranks; deserted Jan. 1, 1899.
Quartermaster-Sergeant Wm. Rauch. Promoted to 1st Sergeant.
Sergeant Cyrus J. Crabbe, Stamford. Discharged Oct. 22d.
Sergeant Henry H. Payne. Reduced to ranks; deserted Jan. 1, 1899.
Sergeant John H. Chase, Kingston, N. Y.
Sergeant Albert H. Buttery. Promoted to 1st Sergeant; reduced to Sergeant.
Corporal Milo C. Brown. Promoted to Sergeant.
Corporal Arthur E. Godfrey. Discharged Feb. 8, 1899.
Corporal Coles M. Flewellin.

Corporal George C. Meehan. Promoted to Quartermaster-Sergeant.
Corporal Ira C. Lockwood. Discharged Dec. 24th.
Corporal Frank H. Webber.
Corporal Frank Neugebauer, So. Norwalk. Reduced to ranks.
Corporal Howard J. Bloomer. Promoted to 2d Lieutenant Co. F, Nov. 14th.
Corporal Edward Brotherton.
Corporal Albert R. Scofield. Reduced to ranks.
Corporal Herbert F. Tuttle. Transferred to band.
Musician Harry S. Richmond. Transferred to band; discharged Dec. 26th.
Musician Frank Eigner, Jr., South Norwalk.

Privates.

Abendroth, Wm. G., South Norwalk. Promoted to Corporal.
Ash, George J., Bridgeport.
Baker, Wm. H., Bridgeport. Deserted Oct. 2d.
Burkedal, Edward
Beagan, John H. Promoted to Corporal.
Brown, Fred
Buttery, Ulysses G.
Britt, Matthew
Bendtzen, Hans C., Westport.
Brennan, David
Butler, Walter A., Wilkesbarre, Pa.
Black, John W., Bridgeport. Deserted Nov. 11th.
Castle, George C.
Cahill, John J.
Connors, George, Bridgeport.
Crawford, James
Cullen, Robert
Cornell, Ernest B.
Chartrand, Nelson H., Shelton.
Canary, John, Bridgeport.
Davis, Charles A.
Durbeck, Emil. Promoted to Corporal.
Donnelly, Wm. Discharged Feb. 1, 1899.
Dougherty, Michael J.
Ellis, Royal A. Discharged Jan. 17, 1899.
Ferris, James, Tarryan, N. Y.
Farrell, Michael, Bridgeport.
Fell, John E.
Flinn, George F. Transferred to Hospital Corps, U. S. A.
Farley, Frank, Bridgeport.
Gorman, John

Godfrey, Frederick W. Discharged Oct. 17th.

Guthrie, Wm. H. Promoted to Corporal.

Hopson, Henry W. Promoted to Corporal.

Hopkins, George W.

Hagerty, Joseph, Bridgeport. Promoted to Corporal.

Hall, Beekman F.

Henry, Joseph F.

Henry, Michael, Bridgeport.

Hadley, Wm. H.

Kinsella, John

Keller, Joe

Kemple, James, Bridgeport. Promoted to Corporal; reduced to ranks.

Keogh, John J.

Kearney, Henry J., Hartford.

Kiley, David, Bridgeport.

Landrigan, Philip J.

Lovejoy, Arthur G.

Law, Sanford B., Stamford. Promoted to Corporal.

Lawlor,. Henry P., Waterbury.

McCarthy, Daniel M., New York.

Murphy, James. Deserted Sept. 8th.

McGuinness, Stephen

McGarry, Thomas J.

Mattmore, Bernard, Worcester, Mass.

Meyers, Wm., Bridgeport.

Morris, Wallace W.

Noyes, Wm. T., New York. Discharged Feb. 2, 1899.

Norman, Arthur S.

O'Brien, Peter F. Promoted to Corporal; reduced to ranks.

Oakes, John W., So. Norwalk.

Osborne, Charles H.

Parker, Charles E.

Phillips, Warden B. Deserted March 3, 1899.

Peterson, John, So. Norwalk.

Peters, John P., Bridgeport. Discharged Feb. 3, 1899.

Quigley, James J., Bridgeport. Appointed Musician.

Rooney, Frank P.

Riley, James A. Promoted to Corporal.

Ross, Thomas H., Harbor Grace, N'f'd.

Sargent, Joseph

Sturm, Joseph F.

Sturm, Valentine. South Norwalk.

Steele, Henry, Waterbury. Appointed Wagoner.

Sullivan, George L.

Sheehan, Wm., South Norwalk.

Shockley, Herbert F.

Storey, Peter

Squires, Joseph, Northampton, Mass.

Smith, Thomas, Bridgeport.

Tetzner, Albert. Promoted to Corporal; promoted to Sergeant.

Troy, William J. Promoted to Corporal.

Tiffany, George B., Bridgeport. Promoted to Corporal.

Valleau, George P., Bridgeport. Discharged Dec. 14th.

Weyerhauser, John P.

Waldorf, Harry M., Bridgeport. Appointed Artificer.

Young, Frank A., Bridgeport.

Company M, of Winsted.

(Co. I, 4th Regiment, C. N. G.)

Captain George M. Crossman. Resigned Sept. 7th.

1st Lieutenant Francis S. Hubbard.

2d Lieutenant, none mustered with Co.

1st Sergeant John H. Parsons. Reduced to ranks; promoted to Corporal.

Quartermaster-Sergeant Edward L. Whiton.

Sergeant Wm. R. Walker.

Sergeant Charles E. Barker. Appointed Chief Musician Regimental Band.

Sergeant Christopher C. Coon, Colebrook.

Sergeant Arthur H. Dean. Reduced to ranks.

Corporal Clarence B. Gillette. Reduced to ranks.

Corporal Charles Clayton. Reduced to ranks.

Corporal Benjamin W. Johnson.

Corporal Edward L. Lynch.

Corporal John J. Simons.

Corporal Orrin W. White, Torrington. Promoted to 1st Sergeant; reduced to Sergeant.

Corporal Martin Crossman.

Corporal Robert B. Crossman. Reduced to ranks.

Corporal Reginald R. Miller.

Corporal Wm. Harrington.

Corporal George E. Doughty. Promoted to Sergeant.

Corporal James T. Grady.

Musician Wilbur F. Beach. Transferred to band.

Musician Joseph H. Wells. Reduced to ranks.

Artificer Eugene P. Searing, Torrington. Promoted to Corporal.

Wagoner John Witzke, Torrington.

Privates.

Amrick, Andrew, Torrington.
Amsbury, John H.
Burke, James, Norwich.
Bertig, Wm. F.
Buck, Charles E.
Beauchamp, Camille J.
Bues, Lowes, Torrington.
Brown, Charles B., Torrington. Appointed Musician.
Brennan, John M.
Barnes, Harry L., Colebrook.
Blythe, Walter. Promoted to Corporal.
Butts, William A.
Centrella, Angelo
Corbette, Louis H.
Caul, Samuel L., Norfolk.
Curtiss, Edward J., Torrington.
Crippen, Homer F., Torrington.
Coons, Daniel, Torrington.
Coons, Harry N., Torrington.
Coons, Louis E., Torrington.
Casey, Charles W., Torrington.
Connole, Patrick F.
Dean, Miles A. Appointed Artificer.
Duplain, George E., Torrington.
Donohue, John
Denison, Silas E., Norwich.
Dean, Miles W., Torrington. Appointed Musician.
Duncan, Wm., Norwich. Discharged Sept. 21st.
Donahue, Michael J.
Donovan, Stephen, Torrington.
Fink, Oluf, Torrington.
Flamer, Emil, Torrington.
Fortin, Samuel, Thompsonville.
Ferencry, Julius
Griffin, Walter N.
Golliker, George, Torrington.
Griffith, Burton D., Torrington. Promoted to Corporal.
Gagne, Joseph A.
Gisselbrecht, Eugene M., Torrington.
Griswold, Grant
Heglin, Samuel, Hartford. Appointed Acting Hospital Steward, N. C. S.
Hine, George I., Torrington. Died Oct. 7th.
Hill, Louis C.
Holland, Daniel
Howard, Dellaware, Norwich. Discharged Sept. 21st.
Hodge, Frank B. Dishonorably discharged.
Hunt, Albert E. Transferred to band.
Judd, Thomas M., Derby. Dishonorably discharged.
Kimberly, Edwin N., Torrington.
Kenney, John J.
Kopankiauritz, Frank, Torrington.
Looby, Michael, Torrington. Dishonorably discharged.
Markwait, Adolph, Torrington.
Monroe, Arthur
Murphy, John
McGrane, James F.
Murphy, Charles, Torrington.
McMahon, John L., Torrington. Dishonorably discharged.
McGrath, Henry
Mitchell, James E. Promoted to Sergeant; promoted to 1st Sergeant.
O'Neil, Michael, Torrington.
O'Connors, Daniel
Padelford, Charles D.
Palmer, Samuel
Ryan, John, Torrington.
Riley, James, Torrington.
Redman, Charles F., Torrington. Promoted to Corporal.
Reardon, Daniel, Torrington.
Rathburn, John H.
Stone, Clifford B.
Stone, Spencer J.
Spitko, Thomas, Torrington.
Stickles, Clayton E., Torrington.
Shea, John J.
Sullivan, James, Torrington.
Sykes, Wilbur H.
Tuozzo, Pasquale, Torrington.
Talbert, Edward, Norfolk. Dishonorably discharged.
Turner, Theodore, Norwich. Discharged Sept. 21st.
Tucker, Patrick, Torrington.
Vibbert, Edward R., Torrington. Promoted to Corporal.
White, Joseph A., Torrington.
Wallace, James, Torrington.
Williams, Walter E., Hartford.
Young, Edward L.

Naval Battalion.

Mustered into the U. S. Service at Niantic, June 15, 1898.

Lieutenant-Commander Arthur H. Day (appointed Lieutenant, U. S. N.), ... New Haven.
Lieutenant Edward V. Raynolds (appointed Lieutenant, U. S. N.), ... New Haven.
Ordnance Officer, Lieutenant (Junior Grade) Nathaniel W. Bishop (appointed Lieutenant, Junior Grade, U. S. N.), ... Bridgeport.
Paymaster, Lieutenant (Junior Grade) Frederick L. Averill (appointed Assistant Paymaster, U. S. N.), ... New Haven.

Non-Commissioned Staff.

Chief Master-at-Arms Charles K. Hutchinson.
Chief Yeoman Henry F. Punderson.

First Division, of New Haven.

Lieutenant Daniel M. Goodridge, New Haven. Appointed Lieutenant (Junior Grade), U. S. N.
Lieutenant (Junior Grade) Frank S. Cornwell, New Haven. Appointed Lieutenant (Junior Grade), U. S. N.
Ensign Stephen D. Baker. Appointed Ensign, U. S. N.
Ensign Robert E. L. Hutchinson, New Haven. Appointed Lieutenant (Junior Grade), U. S. N.

Adams, Henry T., landsman. Discharged Aug. 6, 1898.
Allen, Walter H., seaman. Discharged June 16, 1898. Appointed Naval Cadet U. S. N.
Anketelle, Arthur M., landsman.
Arvine, Earless P., landsman.
Applegate, Wm. A., seaman.
Best, George W., seaman.
Barrett, Harry A., seaman.
Boemer, George F., seaman.
Buzzell, Harry A., seaman.
Burgess, Wm. J., ordinary seaman.
Brown, Arthur H., ordinary seaman.
Brown, Leslie M., landsman.
Benton, Winfred W.
Ball, Benjamin H.
Best, Edward L., seaman.

Bush, Frank W., seaman.
Beach, Joseph W., seaman. Discharged Aug. 6, 1898.
Clemens, Frank G.
Cahill, Wm. J., ordinary seaman.
Church, Ulysses G., landsman.
Cluff, Charles S., landsman.
Carroll, George T., landsman.
Doolittle, Harry W., landsman.
Dusenberre, Ralph E., seaman.
Dulaney, George W., seaman.
Docker, Guy, landsman.
Eldredge, Nathan S., ordinary seaman.
Eels, J. Shepard, ordinary seaman.
Fowler, Frederic C., landsman.
Ferguson, George W., landsman.
Filley, Walter O., ordinary seaman.
Farr, Edward R., ordinary seaman.
Garland, Wm. J., landsman. Discharged August 4, 1898.
Gallagher, Elliot S., landsman.
Heywood, Carl B., ordinary seaman.
Henderson, Yandell. Appointed Ensign U. S. N.
Hamlin, Edgar F., ordinary seaman.
Harger, Alfred M., landsman.
Hott, Frederic, landsman.
Hewett, Wm. H., ordinary seaman.
Huntley, Henry F., seaman.
Hume, Francis S., seaman.
Isbell, John A., ordinary seaman.
Jewett, Ambrose B., landsman.
Judson, Theodore P., ordinary seaman.
Kenyon, Albert J., seaman.
Konitz, Wm. J., seaman.
Kendall, Edward G., ordinary seaman. Discharged Aug. 4, 1898.
Kelsey, Ernest R., ordinary seaman.
Lum, Benjamin B., seaman.

Lee, Charles S., seaman.
Leonard, Harry A., landsman.
Lyons, George, Jr., landsman.
Lewis, Edward Y., seaman.
Lautz, Louis F., landsman.
Lounsbury, Walter W., ordinary seaman.
Lee, Wm. R., landsman.
Murphy, John K., seaman.
Mason, Frank H., seaman.
Makepeace, Walter D., seaman.
Morris, Charles G., seaman.
Nichols, John W., landsman.
Norton, Louis L., ordinary seaman.
O'Brien, James M.
O'Keefe, John A., seaman.
Peck, Clifford M., seaman.
Phillips, Charles C., landsman.
Price, Wm. B., landsman.
Peabody, Robert S., seaman.
Snow, Louis L., ordinary seaman. Discharged Aug. 6, 1898.
Smyth, Nathan A., seaman.
Schurig, Robert C., seaman.
Shepard, E. Morris, landsman. Discharged Aug. 6, 1898.
Scranton, Wm. J., landsman.
Strong, Richard W., landsman.
Trueland, Hiram, seaman.
Woodford, Harry E., landsman.
Williams, Charles E., ordinary seaman.
Way, Charles L., seaman.
Wallace, Edward D., landsman.
Webb, Clarence W., seaman.

Second Division, of Hartford.

Lieutenant Felton Parker. Appointed Lieutenant, U. S. N.
Lieutenant (Junior Grade) Hermann F. Cuntz. Appointed Ensign, U. S. N.
Ensign Louis F. Middlebrook. Appointed Ensign, U. S. N.
Ensign Lyman Root. Appointed Ensign, U. S. N.

Beers, Robert C., landsman.
Berry, Howard, ordinary seaman.
Bigelow, Henry W., seaman. Discharged August 6, 1898.
Baldwin, Henry F., seaman.
Bosworth, Fred E., seaman.
Baxter, George S., seaman.
Blakeslee, Fred G., seaman.
Bissell, Herbert G., seaman.
Brewer, Arthur L., seaman.
Brinley, George, seaman, Newington.
Brinley, John H. W., seaman, Newington.
Buck, Henry R., seaman.

Burke, John F., landsman.
Barber, Arthur W., landsman.
Case, Archibald L., seaman.
Case, Harry B., landsman, Windsor.
Chapin, Robert D., seaman.
Coggeshall, Murry H., seaman.
Cutting, Arthur S., landsman.
Colby, George F., landsman.
Dimock, Stanley K., ordinary seaman. Discharged Aug. 6, 1898.
Doran, Edward J., seaman.
Drury, Henry W., ordinary seaman.
Field, Francis E., seaman.
Forrest, George C., seaman.
Foster, George C., landsman.
Franke, Paul, landsman.
Gabrielle, Burton L., ordinary seaman.
Gallup, Christopher M., seaman. Discharged Aug. 6, 1898.
Geer, Wm. A., landsman.
Gillette, Frank W., ordinary seaman.
Goulet, Wm., landsman.
Hawley, James J., seaman.
Holcombe, George A., ordinary seaman.
Holmes, Richard J., ordinary seaman.
Huntington, Charles A., landsman.
Hurd, Wm. M., ordinary seaman.
Jackson, Edward Q., ordinary seaman.
Kenyon, Lorenzo W., seaman.
Keyes, Frank R., seaman.
Kowalcky, Frank E., landsman.
LeFever, Arthur P., landsman.
Long, Michael C., ordinary seaman. Middletown.
Malm, O. William, seaman.
Martin, George R., ordinary seaman.
McCreary, Ralph W., seaman.
Miller, Guy P., seaman. Discharged Aug. 6, 1898.
Miller, Hugh I., seaman. Discharged Aug. 6, 1898.
Morgan, Victor F., seaman.
Morgan, James H., seaman.
Morris, Shiras, seaman.
Moses, Linwood K., landsman.
McManus, Ward, seaman.
Neilson, Carl, landsman.
Noble, Edward J., ordinary seaman.
Northam, Edward T., seaman. Discharged Aug. 6, 1898.
Northam, Robert C., seaman. Discharged Aug. 3, 1898.
Nutter, Harrie Y., ordinary seaman.
Pynchon, Lauriston F. L., seaman.
Root, Judson B., ordinary seaman.
Sanford, Harrison, ordinary seaman.
Saunders, Charles C., seaman.
Schiberdtfeger, Otto M., landsman.
Scoville, Albert W., Jr., seaman.
Scoville, Lester H., ordinary seaman.
Scrivener, Wm. H., seaman.

Seaver, Frederic A., landsman.
Seymour, Freeman P., ordinary seaman.
Shepherd, Forrest, seaman.
Storrs, Herbert E., seaman.
Talcott, Morton C., landsman.
Twardoks, John F., landsman.
Tregoning, Wm. C., landsman.
Tinkham, George H., landsman.
Uhler, Jonathan K., seaman.
Welles, James D., seaman.
Wilson, Louis B., seaman.
Wightman, Alanson H., seaman.
Wells, Richard B., seaman.
Wilcox, George E., ordinary seaman.
Young, Frank E., landsman.

Engineer Division, of New Haven.

Lieutenant Amasa Trowbridge, Chief Engineer. Appointed Passed Assistant Engineer and Lieutenant (Junior Grade), U. S. N.
Ensign Frederick C. Spencer, Assistant Engineer. Appointed Assistant Engineer and Ensign, U. S. N.

Adams, Francis M., fireman, 1st class.

Anderson, Fred T., fireman, 1st class.
Barrows, George H., fireman, 2d class.
Brown, Curtis P., fireman, 1st class.
Clark, Percival S., fireman, 1st class.
Conroy, Joseph T., coal passer.
Dunlea, Thomas J., Jr., coal passer.
Golden, Edward, coal passer, New York city.
Goodrich, Robert H., fireman, 1st class, Ansonia.
Johnson, George T., fireman, 1st class.
Kondrick, Georg, coal passer, Meriden.
Mahoney, Dennis M., fireman, 1st class.
McMahon, Daniel M., fireman, 1st class.
Minnix, Francis I., fireman, 2d class.
Noonan, Eugene T., coal passer.
Parsons, Arthur L., fireman, 1st class, Ansonia.
Peck, Albert E., coal passer.
Ryan, John P., fireman, 2d class, Hartford.
Ryan, Timothy J., fireman, 2d class.
Ryals, Edward R., fireman, 2d class.
Schatz, Jacob F., fireman, 2d class, Allentown.
Skelly, Henry F., fireman, 2d class.
Tripp, Charles E., coal passer, Shelton.
Wheeler, Lynde P., fireman, 1st class.
Wurts, John C., fireman, 1st class.

In addition to the foregoing, officers from the Connecticut National Guard were appointed in the Volunteers as follows:

Colonel Lucien F. Burpee, Second Regiment, Waterbury, Lieutenant-Colonel and Assistant Judge Advocate, U. S. V.

Lieutenant-Colonel Leonard B. Almy, Medical Director Brigade C. N. G., retired, Norwich, Major and Chief Surgeon, U. S. V.

Lieutenant-Colonel George M. Cole, Third Regiment, New London, Lieutenant-Colonel Fourth Regiment U. S. V.

Colonel James B. Houston, Staff of Commander-in-Chief, Thompsonville, Major and Paymaster, U. S. V.

Captain Benjamin Stark, Jr., Third Regiment, New London, Quartermaster Fourth Regiment U. S. V.

Captain Howard A. Giddings, Brigade Signal Officer, Hartford, Captain and Signal Officer, U. S. V., attached to staff of General Fitzhugh Lee.

1st Lieutenant Wm. F. M. Rogers, 3d Sec. Signal Corps, New London, 1st Lieutenant, U. S. V., Signal Corps, with Gen. Wilson at Porto Rico.

1st Lieutenant Rodmond V. Beach, Battalion Adjutant, Second Regiment, New Haven, 1st Lieutenant and Adjutant First Regiment U. S. V. Engineers, died at Porto Rico Sept. 28, 1898.

Ex-Captain Wm. C. Dwight, Co. K, First Regiment, Hartford, Major and Paymaster U. S. V.

Captain Frederick A. Hill, Co. F, Fourth Regiment, Norwalk, Major and Judge Advocate U. S. V.

Lieutenant Philip E. Fairfield, commanding 1st Sec. Brigade Signal Corps C. N. G., Hartford, Sergeant-Major U. S. V. Signal Corps Battalion, died at Jacksonville, Fla., Oct. 28, 1898.

The following enlisted men from the Brigade Signal Corps served in the Signal Corps, U. S. Volunteers:

Michael F. Owen, Hartford, promoted to Sergeant.

Fred C. Morcom, Hartford, promoted to Sergeant.

Samuel A. Gager, New London, promoted to Sergeant.

Harry C. Platt, New London, promoted to Sergeant.

Anton E. Sauter, New London, promoted to Sergeant.

William Lounsbury, Bridgeport, promoted to Sergeant.

Frederick A. Mackenzie, Hartford, promoted to Sergeant.

Alec York Stilson, New Haven, promoted to Corporal.

George C. Fuller, Bridgeport, promoted to Corporal.